The Leader's Guide to
The Relaxation & Stress Reduction Workbook

Fifth Edition

Martha Davis, Ph.D.

New Harbinger Publications, Inc.

Publisher's Note

Distributed in the U.S.A. by Publishers Group West; in Canada by Raincoast Books; in Great Britain by Airlift Book Company, Ltd.; in South Africa by Real Books, Ltd.; in Australia by Boobook; and in New Zealand by Tandem Press.

Copyright © 2001 by   Martha Davis
                      New Harbinger Publications, Inc.
                      5674 Shattuck Avenue
                      Oakland, CA 94609

Cover design by Shelby Design and Illustrates
Edited by Heather Garnos
Text design by Spencer Smith

ISBN 1-57224-233-7 Paperback

New Harbinger Publications' Web site address: www.newharbinger.com

03   02   01

10   9   8   7   6   5   4   3   2   1

First printing

Contents

Preface

This guide was specifically designed to assist you in leading groups, using *The Relaxation & Stress Reduction Workbook*. It tells you

- the salient points in teaching stress reduction and relaxation.

- which are the most important exercises to cover, and which are optional.

- a logical order for presenting the exercises.

- the length of time needed for each exercise.

- what materials are needed for each exercise.

- how to integrate *The Relaxation & Stress Reduction Workbook* audiotapes into your program.

- several formats for different lengths of groups.

- the typical problems people encounter when first learning these techniques and suggestions for resolving them.

- how to adjust exercises to fit your group size and environmental specifications.

- how to give clear homework assignments.

- how to review homework in group.

- how to use resistance as a teaching tool.

- how to motivate students to do their homework and continue to use these techniques when the group is over.

This guide assumes that you are already familiar with *The Relaxation & Stress Reduction Workbook*, so it will not repeat the basic concepts and step-by-step instructions found there. For best results, have your students read the workbook as the text used for your class or workshop. The short lectures and exercises you give them in class will then be reinforced by their reading at home.

It is important for you to add material that is of particular interest to you and to your specific group. This will bring special meaning and vitality to the material, and will keep the group and you fresh and involved.

Refer to the bibliography at the end of each chapter in the workbook. Feel free to experiment with and expand upon the material presented here and in the workbook.

1

Introduction to Relaxation and Stress Reduction

One of the best ways to begin the class is to introduce yourself; talk briefly about how you became interested in the field of stress management and relaxation, what experience you have in teaching this subject, and why you think this is an important topic for the people in your class.

Stress and the Stress Response

Your introduction leads naturally into a brief lecture on stress and the stress response. Be sure to highlight the basic concepts of chapter 1 in the workbook and include points of relevancy for your particular audience.

Time: 30 minutes

Special Notes

Here are several important points to keep in mind when you give a lecture to the class:

1. The three major purposes of a lecture in this context are **to inform, to clarify misconceptions,** and **to motivate.**

2. Give new information in small chunks so that people can easily assimilate it.

3. Keep your message simple. The average audience will not be interested in nor remember more than a few cited research studies. While you will want to provide some historical context and a scientific basis for the importance of stress management and relaxation, you will lose a lot of people if you give them an academic treatise.

4. Gear your message to the educational level and interests of your audience.

5. Make your message encouraging. Cite personal or clinical anecdotes and studies that indicate that your concepts are grounded in experience and that your techniques work.

6. Provide an opportunity for class members to ask questions. It's best if you let people know before you start lecturing whether you want to answer their questions as you go along or at the end of your talk.

7. Make it clear before you start answering questions that the purpose of a stress management and relaxation class is to teach general concepts and techniques that have universal relevancy, and not to address the details of an individual's particular life situation. It is hoped that in the process of learning these general skills the individual will solve many of his own specific problems or clarify the need for one-on-one professional help.

8. Since the individual student will relate to the general concepts and techniques in terms of his specific situation, he will often bring up questions and comments particular to his life experience. This can benefit him and the class as long as it throws further light on the basic stress management concepts and exercises. However, it is important for the leader to interrupt people who want to talk at length about their symptoms and problems. You can relate these individual examples to general stress management concepts, and then redirect the class to stress management skill building. Examples of how to do this are as follows:

   "That brings up an important point, Mrs. Cook." Then follow up this statement with how her problem or symptom is a good example of stress or a stress response.

   *

   "You sound pretty discouraged, frustrated, and angry about the unfair treatment you are getting at work. What stress management tools have you learned thus far that you think might help you deal more effectively with your reaction to this stress?"

   *

   "You must be my straight man today, John, I was just about to bring up the topic of 'Job Stress.'"

   *

   "Betty, I know that your husband and children really get on your nerves, and you have discovered that the stress reduction technique of just talking about it reduces your frustration level and tension headaches. Rather than use the group to ventilate your feelings, I'd like to see you begin to make some new friends with whom you can share your feelings and get emotional support. Social networks serve as a buffer against the stresses of life."

9. At some point during the first session, you may want to give the class logistical information. This information can be in written form and referred to in as little or as much detail as you prefer. Typical logistical information includes:

   • the name of your class or workshop

- your name
- when the class session is to begin and end
- the total number of sessions
- the date of the last session
- holidays when the class will not meet
- when you plan to take a break during the session
- location of rest rooms and smoking areas
- your expectations regarding confidentiality
- your expectations regarding audiotaping
- your expectations regarding attendance and punctuality
- your expectations regarding class participation
- your expectations regarding homework assignments
- instructions regarding how to get credit for the class
- requirements for those taking class for credit
- name of text and where it can be purchased
- list of topics to be covered
- the learning modalities to be used:

    lecture

    demonstration of exercises

    practice exercises in class

    discussion and questions

    practice exercises at home

    monitoring your own experience and progress

    reading text at home

    audio cassette tapes

10. At this point, the group members are clear about what they are going to learn, why you think that it is important, and how you intend to conduct the class.

Exercise: Schedule of Recent Experience

Purpose:

1. Allows individuals to get acquainted.

2. Enables individuals to acknowledge to themselves and others the major stresses in their lives.

3. Underscores the relationship between cumulative stress and the possibility of major illness.

Time: 30 minutes

Materials: If students do not have their own copies of *The Relaxation & Stress Reduction Workbook* yet, give each group member a copy of the Schedule of Recent Experience sheets on pages 3 to 7. Provide extra pencils or pens for those who do not have one.

Instructions:

1. You can use the introduction to the Schedule of Recent Experience on page 3 in the workbook. Remind the class that one definition of stress is "any change to which you have to adjust."

2. Go over the instructions on page 3 in the workbook, and then answer questions.

3. Tell students to raise their hand if they have a question as they go along, and you will come over and assist them.

4. Go over the instructions for scoring on page 6 in the workbook, and then answer the questions.

5. When everybody is finished scoring the inventory, call the class back to order.

6. If you are working with a large group, have students break into small groups of three or four people, introduce themselves, and share what they have learned about themselves in taking the Schedule of Recent Experience. Have one person in each group volunteer to later report back to the large group anything particularly interesting or any unanswered questions that come up in her group. (If you are working with a small group, you can ask each person to share in turn.)

7. Two minutes before the end of the allotted time, give people a two-minute warning to wrap it up.

8. Have the small groups reassemble into one large group. Then ask each one of the small group reporters to share what her group learned that was particularly interesting and any questions that remained unanswered. During this discussion, be sure that the following points are covered:

   - Changes can be big or small, positive and/or negative.

   - Having to adapt to change is stressful.

   - The stress of change is cumulative.

   - The amount of change a person experiences may be predictive of future illness.

   - People vary in their perception of a given life event and their ability to adapt to it.

- Just because a person received a high score doesn't mean that he has to get sick; the individual can do many things to help prevent illness and stay healthy.

Other points to include:

- The range of scores given for the Schedule of Recent Experience is based on a hospital population. Persons who received high scores were people who tended to get sick more frequently than people with low scores. This is only a correlation. Critics of the Schedule of Recent Experience would argue that it does not necessarily show cause. There are many other factors that contribute to whether a person is likely to become ill, such as genetic predisposition, stabilizing influences (i.e., a good social network, a pleasant home life, a satisfying job, a regular exercise program), and how people perceive the stresses in their lives and their ability to respond to those stresses.

- Typically, there will be a few participants who will score low on the Schedule of Recent Experience but who are ill or worn out. Have these people fill out the inventory again, this time for the year preceding the past year. It is likely that their second score will be higher than their first. A frequent comment from these people is that they really needed this class one or two years ago, but were too busy just trying to survive.

- Since we cannot change our genetic inheritance or our past experience, stress management focuses on what we do have some control over: our thoughts, feelings and behavior, and to a lesser extent, our environment.

Symptom Checklist

Purpose:

1. This inventory will help individuals identify their stress symptoms and decide how uncomfortable each of these symptoms are.

2. At the end of class, students can fill out the checklist a second time to determine how much symptom relief they were able to achieve with the tools they learned in this class.

Time: 10 to 20 minutes

Instructions:

1. See pages 7 and 8 in the workbook.

2. This inventory can be filled out in class or given as homework.

3. After your students have completed this inventory, call for questions and comments.

4. *Optional:* Read off the symptoms and have people raise their hand if they gave themselves a three or higher on a particular item. This is useful information for you. It will

also give your students a sense that they are not alone in their particular brand of suffering.

5. *Optional*: Let people form dyads to briefly discuss their symptoms of stress. Limit this to about four minutes.

Tactics for Coping with Stress Inventory

Purpose:

This inventory enables individuals to identify how they typically cope with stressful events, assess whether their behavior patterns are constructive, and begin to consider trying out constructive tactics.

Time: 10 minutes

Instructions:

1. See pages 9 and 10 in the workbook.

2. This inventory can be filled out in class or given as homework. It only takes a couple of minutes. Remind your students that they should fill it out in terms of what they actually do and not what they think they *should* be doing.

3. Ask people to total the number of even-numbered items they checked and then total the number of odd-numbered items they checked. After this is completed, remind the group that the less constructive tactics for coping with stress are the odd-numbered items: 1, 3, 5, and so forth…. The more constructive tactics for coping with stress are the even numbers.

4. Since people like to know how they compare on this inventory to others, you may want to ask for a show of hands of people who checked five or more even-numbered items. You can have them leave their hands up if they checked six or more even-numbered items and so forth. Congratulate people for already using many of the more constructive tactics. You may want to ask for a show of hands of people who checked five or more odd-num bered items. You can have them leave their hands up if they checked six or more odd-numbered items and so forth. You can encourage people to try out some of the constructive tactics they are not currently using and consider changing some of their less constructive tactics.

5. You can generate group discussion by pointing out that not all of the odd-numbered items are necessarily bad nor are all of the even-numbered items necessarily good. Ask for some examples to illustrate this.

6. This is a good time to mention the research on "stress-hardy" individuals and the difference between "type A" personalities and "type B" personalities discussed on page 9 of the workbook.

Symptom Effectiveness Chart

Purpose:

1. This chart gives a rough overview of the most effective stress management and relaxation techniques for relieving specific symptoms.

2. This is an excellent way to give a quick overview of what you plan to cover in your course.

3. It is interesting to review this chart with the class at the last session, asking individuals which tools they thought were most useful in relieving their stress symptoms. This can be done efficiently with a show of hands. This discussion provides useful information for you to consider how you will improve your classes in the future.

Time: 5 minutes

Instructions:

1. See pages 11 to 13 in the workbook.

2. Show your students how to read the chart.

Note: While the techniques that are most effective in treating a specific symptom are marked with an "X," students must take into account their individual situation in deciding which tools will help them. For example, Lonnie's major symptom of stress is obesity due to compulsive eating. Obviously, she needs to work on nutrition and exercise. But she also needs to ask *what triggers* her compulsive eating. If she eats because she is a perfectionist who often fails to achieve her high expectations, she needs to look at "Refuting Irrational Ideas" (chapter 12). If she eats because she has difficulty saying "no" to people, asking directly for what she wants, dealing with criticism from others, or expressing her feelings and opinions, then she needs some "Assertiveness Training" (chapter 17). If she tends to give up her diet or exercise program at the first temptation or hardship, she will benefit from "Coping Skills Training" (chapter 15). If she eats to relax and dampen her anxiety, then she would benefit from learning relaxation techniques. The Stress Awareness Diary, in "Body Awareness" (chapter 2), is a useful tool for students who want to learn more about what triggers their symptoms of stress.

2

Body Awareness

Exercise: Body Inventory

Purpose: Promotes awareness of body, especially tension areas.

Time: about 25 minutes

Instructions:

1. See pages 15 to 20 in the workbook.

2. Give a brief introduction to Body Awareness.

3. These exercises can be done sitting up or lying down. Instruct people to loosen any constricting clothing, take everything off their laps, uncross their arms and legs, remove their glasses or contacts if they like, and get into a comfortable position. This a good reminder to give when teaching any relaxation exercise.

4. Suggest that people close their eyes to make it easier to focus inward. Or if they prefer, they can pick a comfortable spot on the floor or wall to gently rest their eyes.

5. Lead the group through the Internal versus External Awareness exercise, pausing after each step to give people time to inwardly respond. In a similar manner, continue on with Body Scanning and Letting Go of Your Body.

6. After completing these three exercises, suggest that the group take a moment to open their eyes and gradually come back into the room. After people have had a few moments to reorient, ask a few questions to encourage them to talk about their experiences with these exercises in the large group or in dyads.

7. These three exercises are presented in this order because they build on one another and ask the participant to do progressively more challenging things. The exercises

can, however, be presented separately or in conjunction with other relaxation exercises. If you have time to do only one of these exercises, do Body Scanning.

8. *Optional*: Rather than leading the group through the exercises yourself, you may prefer to play the 21-minute New Harbinger Publications audio cassette tape on Body Inventory, which includes Awareness, Body Scanning, and Letting Go of Your Body.

9. Encourage people to practice these three Body Inventory exercises each day on their own. Good times to practice are when they go to bed, before getting up in the morning, when they have to wait, during a work break, or any other naturally occurring lull during their day when they are free to turn their attention inward. The other option is to schedule an appointment with themselves to do a Body Inventory each day at a particular time.

10. Tell members to use the Record of General Tension described on workbook page 19 to keep track of their tension level before and after they do Body Inventory exercises. In this way, they can monitor their progress and remind themselves to do the exercises regularly.

11. *Optional:* Have your students use the Record of General Tension to monitor their progress on all relaxation homework assignments.

Exercise: Stress Awareness Diary

Purpose:

1. The diary is a homework tool that allows students to monitor their awareness of their symptoms and stresses throughout the day.

2. The diary identifies how particular stresses result in predictable symptoms.

Time: 5 minutes to explain in class

Materials: several pieces of paper and a pen or pencil

Instructions:

1. Have the participants follow the instructions in the workbook on pages 17 and 18.

2. Many people find that it is excessive to keep the diary for two weeks. Students who keep a diary for two or three days during a week and one day on the weekend net some very useful data. For this exercise, it is best to set a minimal expectation for homework, and let people exceed it.

3. Tell your students that they will have an opportunity to go over their Body Inventory exercises and Stress Awareness Diary at the beginning of the next session.

4. Start the next session by having participants gather in groups of three or four to discuss how each person fared with the assignments.

- Instruct the people who did their assignments to describe any connections they observed between specific stresses in their lives and their symptoms of stress. Ask them also to comment on their experience with the Awareness exercises and their Record of General Tension.

- See chapter 22 in this guide for suggestions on how to deal with people who do not do their homework.

- When the large group is reconvened, have one member from each small group report on how many people did the homework, and any interesting observations or unanswered questions.

3

Breathing

Exercise: Breathing Awareness and Deep Breathing

Purpose:

1. Enables a person to discover how she currently breathes.

2. Points out the most obvious bad breathing habits.

3. Develops awareness of how the chest, diaphragm, and abdomen each play a role in the breathing process.

4. Facilitates deep, relaxing breathing.

Time: 20 minutes

Instructions:

1. Perhaps because people take breathing for granted, starting with a lecture about breathing is a waste of time. Here is an effective way to capture people's attention and bring it to their breathing. Say to your audience, "Before we talk about breathing, I want you to focus your attention on my finger for a moment." Point your index finger into the air at shoulder height and wave it back and forth about eight times. When you stop, immediately ask, "How many of you stopped breathing while you watched my finger? Raise your hands. How many of you don't know if you stopped breathing? Raise your hands." Typically about two-thirds of the audience will acknowledge that they stopped breathing during your finger waving. Point out that your finger waving was a relatively neutral stimulus and that many far less neutral stimuli catch their attention throughout their day, causing them to temporarily stop breathing or to breathe shallowly in the upper part of their chests.

2. Follow the instructions for the Breathing Awareness exercise on pages 23 and 24 in the workbook. Ideally, this exercise should be done lying down, in loose clothing, and on a blanket or rug on the floor. If this is not possible, have participants do the exercise in their seats.

3. Move around the room to make sure that people have their hands placed correctly. Share your observations regarding individuals' breathing patterns (i.e., breath holding, shallow chest breathing, and deep abdominal breathing). Invite questions and comments.

4. After your students are all aware of how they typically breathe, demonstrate Diaphragmatic, or Abdominal, Breathing while in a sitting and lying down pose (see pages 24 and 25 in the workbook). Place one hand on your chest and one hand on your abdomen, exhale deeply, pause, and inhale slowly. Exaggerate the movement so that it is easy for your students to see. Demonstrate pressing down on your abdomen as you exhale to force air out. When you are lying down, rest a book on your abdomen to illustrate exhalation and inhalation. Note that Diaphragmatic Breathing is generally easier to practice initially when lying down, and that they can experiment with the lying down and sitting up poses at home.

5. Instruct your students to shift to Diaphragmatic, or Abdominal, Breathing by exhaling completely, pausing a moment, and then inhaling slowly. Have them keep one hand on their chest and one hand on their abdomen to feel the falling and rising motion of their breath emptying and filling their lungs. To further encourage abdominal breathing, suggest that they press one hand down on their abdomen as they exhale and let their abdomen push the hand back up as they inhale deeply. Invite questions and comments, point out your observations of their breathing patterns, and make suggestions for improvement as needed.

    A common complaint is that Diaphragmatic, or Abdominal, Breathing feels unnatural and awkward. Assure your students that breathing like this is like learning to ride with training wheels on a bicycle: at first they are very conscious of having to get the feel of and master the various aspects of their new skill. With practice, riding a bike and Diaphragmatic Breathing become one automatic, continuous motion. The training wheels come off the bike, and there is no longer a need to exaggerate the Diaphragmatic Breathing. They need to be patient. They have had a lifetime of breathing incorrectly; suggest that it will take them a while to learn to breathe correctly.

6. Go on to instruction 4 of the Deep Breathing exercise on page 25 of the workbook. Assure people that it is all right to breathe through their mouth if they are unable to breathe through their nose. Then have your students practice instruction 5 of the Deep Breathing exercise for a few minutes.

7. Instruct your students to continue practicing Deep Breathing while you tell them about the importance breathing plays in their lives. This is a good time to go back to the introduction on breathing that you skipped (see pages 21 and 22 in the workbook).

8. Begin to draw the breathing exercise to a close by suggesting they do steps 6 through 9 of the Deep Breathing exercise. Then ask your students to take a moment to stretch and come back into the room. Invite questions and comments.

Note: This can be the natural point for a break or end of class.

Breathing to Release Tension

Purpose: To relax. While people almost always find Diaphragmatic, or Deep Breathing, very relaxing, they find that their minds begin to wander after a few minutes—to daydreams, worries, memories, or plans—and they forget to breathe deeply and relax. The following two exercises provide a focus for the mind.

Time: 10 minutes per exercise

1. Breath Counting (see page 26 in the workbook)
   A. Explain and demonstrate (count your exhalations aloud up to four and begin again at one). State that it's all right if their minds wander. In fact, it is to be expected. When they catch themselves straying from counting their exhalations, they are simply to bring their minds back to "one" as they exhale. Always invite questions before moving on to the practice, since no matter how clearly you explain this exercise, somebody doesn't get it.
   B. Have your students take everything out of their laps, uncross their legs and arms, close their eyes if they like, breathe diaphragmatically, and practice this exercise for five minutes.
   C. Invite questions and comments about their experience and the technique.

   Note: This is a favorite exercise among students that is easy to learn and gives some immediate release of tension. If you only have a brief amount of time to devote to breathing, you might want to include this exercise after instruction 7 of Deep Breathing above. There is a more detailed breath counting meditation in the Meditation chapter of the workbook.

2. Letting Go of Tension (see page 26 in the workbook)
   A. Explain and demonstrate this exercise (think out loud). Invite questions about the instructions.
   B. Have your students practice this exercise for five minutes.
   C. Invite questions and comments about their experience and the technique.

Breathing for Symptom Control or Release (Optional)

- see pages 27 to 30 in the workbook

- Abdominal Breathing and Imagination show how breathing techniques can be combined with mental pictures to enhance energy, reduce pain, and assist in the healing process.

- Alternative Breathing is extremely relaxing and particularly effective in relieving tension and sinus headaches. The one problem with this exercise is that it requires relatively clear nasal passages. Have people do this exercise as slowly and gently as they can. It is unlikely class members will do this exercise unless you demonstrate it to them, because the instructions, while simple, appear complex.

- Breath Training for people who hyperventilate.

- Controlled Breathing describes how to make a breath training tape if individuals in your group find Breath Training difficult.

Special Notes

1. Demonstrate each of the breathing exercises as you describe them.

2. Repeat the instructions two or three times while people are practicing these exercises.

3. Walk around the room and identify and correct obvious problems individuals are having.

4. At the completion of each exercise, answer questions about that exercise before going on to the next one.

5. Have group members keep track of their tension levels on their Record of General Tension forms before and after their home relaxation practice sessions.

Audiotape

The New Harbinger Publications 18-minute cassette tape *Breathing* is divided into four segments, which you can use to teach the following exercises:

1. Deep Breathing

2. Two short energizing breathing exercises

3. Complete Natural Breathing

4. Alternative Breathing

4

Progressive Relaxation

Exercise: Progressive Relaxation

Purpose: Deep relaxation without the aid of imagination or will power. All it takes is simple, mechanical tensing and relaxing of major muscle groups.

Time: about 30 minutes

Instructions:

1. The instructions in the workbook on pages 32 to 33 are quite complete.

2. *Optional:* You can use the 22-minute audio cassette *Progressive Relaxation* by New Harbinger Publications to take the class through Progressive Relaxation. This way you are free to demonstrate the technique as the tape describes what to do. You are also able to walk around the room during the exercise and correct individual problems.

3. *Optional:* You can model your own presentation of Progressive Relaxation on the audio cassette. This will help you establish proper timing.

Special Notes

While Progressive Relaxation can be practiced in a chair, it is best to practice in a recliner, in bed, or on a comfortable rug or blanket on the floor. The reason is that when you instruct a person to let go, they ideally should be able to let go without worrying about hitting a hard surface, hurting themselves, placing their hands on their legs, or making a loud noise. Make clear to your students sitting in chairs that they are learning this technique in a less than ideal setting, and that it will be much easier to do at home.

You will need to move around the room and observe each person practicing this exercise in order to make corrections.

The most obvious mistake that people make when they are first learning this technique is to slowly bring their arms or legs down. This is an indication that they are not letting go of the tension in their arms. This is easily corrected by you demonstrating, using exaggeration, "letting go" of your arm tension in a *controlled* slow way and then "letting go" by letting your arm fall *limply* to your side. Let them try to do it correctly immediately .

Encourage people who do not tense enough to tense more, and suggest to those who are obviously overly straining to tense less.

Tell class members to be cautious with any part of their body that has been previously injured or is otherwise weakened. Pain is an indication that they are tensing too hard.

Reassure people that tingling, jerking, needlelike sensations, "surging," and warmth are all normal sensations associated with tensing and relaxing.

After you have taken the group through the basic procedure of Progressive Relaxation, have participants form dyads for three minutes of sharing. Answer questions when the groups combine into one.

Encourage people to practice Progressive Relaxation twice a day for 15 minutes. Almost all participants express some immediate benefit from this exercise, and within a week or two most people report attaining profound relaxation in less than 15 minutes.

Have group members keep track of their level of tension on the 10-point scale described on page 19 in the workbook before and after they do Progressive Relaxation at home.

Once people have mastered the long form of Progressive Relaxation (this usually takes a week or two), have them practice the short form twice a day.

When students have mastered the short form of Progressive Relaxation, suggest that they use it at times during the day when they are tense: when they are waiting, during a mini work break, before they start driving, after a stressful interaction, or before they go to sleep.

This is a powerful relaxation exercise and easy to learn. It should be included in any abbreviated stress management program.

People who are in physical pain due to injury, disease, or extreme tension often prefer a gentler form of Progressive Relaxation called Release-Only Relaxation, described on pages 63 and 64 of the workbook.

5

Meditation

Introduction

Purpose: Meditation in which the individual attempts to focus his attention on one thing at a time can be a profound form of deep relaxation for the mind as well as the body.

Time: 5 minutes

Instructions:

1. See pages 35 and 37 in the workbook.

2. As with breathing, it is more important for people to experience meditation than understand it intellectually. However, focusing on one thing at a time seems foreign and difficult to Westerners. So a brief introduction to meditation will help to familiarize your group with the fundamental elements common to all forms of meditation, as well as the psychological, and physiological benefits of it.

Environment: People can practice meditation on the floor, on cushions, or in chairs. Soft lighting and a comfortable room temperature are ideal. A quiet atmosphere is preferred, but not necessary. Suggest that extraneous sounds are part of the natural environment to be noted and then let go of.

Establishing Your Posture and Centering Yourself

Time: 5 minutes

Instructions:

1. See pages 37 to 39 in the workbook.

2. Demonstrate as you explain the various positions for meditation. If you are not experienced with the full lotus position, do not attempt to demonstrate or teach it. If convenient, have your group practice each of these positions with you. If space is limited, it is fine for your group to practice proper posture in their chairs.

3. Once your students are comfortable in their chosen position, describe or read aloud the directions for Centering Yourself. Move directly to one of the three basic meditations.

Group 1. Three Basic Meditations

Time: 30 minutes

Instructions:

1. Mantra Meditation practiced aloud as a group can be a powerful first meditation experience. Refer to the instructions in the workbook on page 40. First demonstrate chanting "OM" and then lead the group in chanting aloud "OM" for a few minutes. Then have the group silently chant "OM" for a few minutes. Ask participants to compare for themselves the difference in their body between chanting aloud versus in silence. Ask which is more relaxing.

2. The Sitting Meditation, described on page 41 of the workbook, is not as simple as the workbook implies. In fact, most students find it very challenging as they discover what chatterboxes their minds are when they attempt to focus simply on their breath. To lessen their discouragement, point out that distracting thoughts are an essential part of this exercise. Without them, the meditator would not have the opportunity to strengthen his mental discipline each time he brings his attention gently back to his breath.

3. The Breath-Counting Meditation, outlined on page 41 of the workbook, is a variation on the sitting meditation. You may choose to teach just one of these two exercises. Both are excellent means of practicing impartial awareness in the present moment.

4. As your students discuss their experiences with practicing the Basic Meditations, weave in the items from the Special Considerations on page 42 of the workbook that seem to apply.

5. *Optional:* Form small groups of three or four to let people discuss their experiences with these meditative experiences. Which did they like the most and why? What difficulties did they encounter? How did they deal with them? After five minutes, have the groups assemble into one group and let each group representative give a brief summary of the important points and questions brought up. Address any unresolved questions.

6. Suggest that your students select one of these forms of meditation to practice 10 to 20 minutes, once or twice a day for a week, and then decide if they want to continue this form of meditation or try another.

Group 2. Releasing Muscular Tension

Time: up to 5 minutes each

These exercises are essentially Body Awareness exercises. You may choose to include them when you discuss Body Awareness. They are optional meditation exercises. See the instructions in the workbook on pages 42 to 44.

Group 3. Mindfulness and Present Moment Awareness

These are three optional exercises that teach the individual to focus his attention on the here and now. These exercises can be practiced anywhere, but for best results they initially should be practiced with minimal disturbances. The instructions for these exercises are simple to follow. They are in the workbook on pages 44 to 46. You may choose to do the Walking Meditation with the class, if you have the space. For, eating meditation, provide wedges of oranges or other fresh fruit. Suggest that individuals try these meditations on their own in their daily life and then report back to class in the next session what their experiences were like.

Group 4. Mindfulness of Pain or Discomfort

Time: up to 5 minutes each

The Don't Move Exercise is especially useful in suggesting a way to deal with uncomfortable feelings and sensations that are bound to come up during meditation, or for that matter, any time. See the instructions in the workbook on pages 47 to 48.

Group 5. Letting Go of Thoughts

This is a powerful exercise that teaches the individual to observe her flow of consciousness without becoming caught up in it. It underscores the unruly nature of our minds: how thoughts and sensations appear seemingly from nowhere and become all-consuming if we let ourselves dwell on them. It is suggested as an optional exercise because most people find it difficult, and few stay with it long enough to experience its benefits. The instructions for this exercise are on page 48 of the workbook.

Special Note

Suggest to your students that they can gradually expand the practice time of each of these exercises as feels comfortable. See "A Word about Time" on page 39 in the workbook.

Audiotape

The New Harbinger cassette tape *Meditation* is 38 minutes long. It is based on the first edition of *The Relaxation & Stress Reduction Workbook* and does not closely adhere to the Meditation chapter in the fifth edition. It includes the following ten segments:

1. Introduction to Meditation

2. Posture, Centering, Scanning for Tension, and Letting Go

3. Yoga Awareness Exercise

4. Problem Solving

5. Breath Counting

6. Mantra Meditation

7. Contemplation

8. Yantra Meditation

9. Lotus of a Thousand Petals

10. Visualizing One Thing at a Time

6

Visualization

Introduction

Purpose: This chapter would have been better named "Imagination," for it describes how to use all of your senses to tap your own creative resources for guidance, healing, stress reduction, and relaxation.

Time: 5 minutes

Instructions:

1. See pages 51 to 53 in the workbook.

2. When introducing this topic, you will probably want to mention some of the fascinating work of Emil Coué, Carl Jung, Stephanie Matthews, O. Carl Simonton, and others. Briefly describe the three different kinds of visualization, as well as the rules for effective visualization.

Basic Tension and Relaxation Exercises

Present the three basic tension and relaxation exercises: Eye Relaxation, Metaphorical Images, and Creating Your Special Place; and the two optional exercises: Finding Your Inner Guide and Listening to Music.

1. Eye Relaxation (Palming)

Time: 5 minutes

Instructions: See page 54 in the workbook.

Note: Many people assume that they are not imaginative and therefore will perform poorly on the visualization exercises. This is a good visualization exercise to begin with, because it does not rely on imagination. Rather, it allows the individual to relax and observe natural phenomena. Hence, it's almost impossible for anyone to "fail" with this exercise.

2. Metaphorical Images

Time: 8 minutes

Instructions: See page 54 in the workbook.

Note: Here is a slight variation on the instructions given in the workbook. Have your students describe to themselves an uncomfortable place in their bodies which they would like to make feel better. Tell your students to select a tension image that really captures the essence of their tense or painful area. (For instance, a burning, stabbing sensation might bring to mind a sword of dry ice.) Then instruct your students to come up with an image that will greatly reduce or eliminate the tension or pain. Finally, let the two images interact so that the image of tension or pain is diminished, or gotten rid of, by the image of relief. For example, the sun shining brightly on the sword of dry ice as it evaporates. Have your students share their images in groups of four or ask for examples in the large group.

3. Creating Your Special Place

Time: 10 minutes

Instructions: See pages 55 to 56 of the workbook.

Note: Tell your students that their special place may be a real place where they have experienced feeling completely relaxed and safe; or it can be a creation of their imagination. Also mention that they may see, hear, taste, smell, and feel their special place in detail, or they may just have a strong general sense of being there. What is important is that they experience and enjoy their special place in their own unique way.

4. Finding Your Inner Guide

Time: 8 minutes

Instructions: See page 56 of the workbook.

Note: This is an optional exercise. While everybody seems to have a positive response to their special place, some people are frightened or saddened by this exercise. This latter group of individuals typically imagine guides who are dead or not to be trusted. Thus, it's a good idea not to combine the two exercises the first time that you teach Creating Your Special Place.

The value of tapping into one's inner guide cannot be underestimated. The people who have difficulties with Finding Your Inner Guide will either work them through or discontinue using this exercise.

An alternative to Finding Your Inner Guide that does not generate negative feelings is Receptive Visualization, found on pages 52 and 53 of the workbook. Tell your students that they must be patient with these exercises, and may have to practice them for a while before receiving any guidance.

5. Listening to Music

Optional Instructions: See pages 56 to 57 of the workbook.

Note: Because listening to music is such an important and easy way to relax, you will want to introduce your students to various types of relaxing recorded sounds, including natural sounds. You can play music before and after class and during breaks. You can use soft background music while teaching some of the relaxation exercises or while your students are filling out questionnaires. Let your class know what you are playing and where they can purchase it. If invited, your students will quickly expand your knowledge of "relaxing sounds."

Special Notes

1. You need to reiterate to your class the three suggestions (A, B, and C) on page 57 of the workbook. The remainder of this chapter is optional.

2. Laughter is an excellent form of tension release. In addition to the humor exercise suggested on page 57 of the workbook, you may want to demonstrate the power of humor by telling a few jokes, sharing an amusing human interest story, or playing part of an audiotape of one of your favorite comics. Encourage your students to look at the humorous side of their problems.

3. A creative outlet can relieve stress and tension. Many adults put aside playing music, writing, painting, or doing crafts long ago in order to meet obligations and get ahead. The exercise, taken from *Drawing on the Right Side of the Brain*, is a good homework assignment that will demonstrate the relaxing effect of the creative process. It is described on pages 58 of the workbook. Ask your students who have a creative outlet how it affects their tension level. Suggest to them that they take up an old creative interest, or discover a new one for themselves.

Audiotape

The New Harbinger Publications 21-minute cassette tape on *Imagination* is based on the first edition of *The Relaxation & Stress Reduction Workbook* and does not closely adhere to the chapter in the fifth edition. Use it to get additional ideas for Visualization exercises. Play portions of it for your students in lieu of taking them through the Visualization exercises yourself. It is divided into the following segments:

1. Introduction to Imagination as a stress reduction relaxation tool

2. Metaphorical images

3. Change pain by pushing it away or changing its size or shape

4. Body scan for tension, which is red, and relaxation, which is blue; turn all to blue

5. Images of warmth for relaxation

6. Putting down the tension and stress in your life on a mountain path, on the way to your special place

7. Active remembering and then letting go

8. Finding an ally

7

Applied Relaxation Training

Introduction

Purpose: This is a progressive program that teaches the individual to relax both mind and body in stressful situations in only 20 or 30 seconds.

Time: 5 weeks of twice daily practice

Instructions:

1. See pages 61 to 67 in the workbook.

2. Briefly describe the purpose of Applied Relaxation Training, why it was developed, and its five stages (see pages 61 and 62 in the workbook).

3. Since this is a progressive program, it is very important that the individual master one stage before moving on to the next. It takes about a week or two of twice daily practice to become comfortable enough with one stage to feel ready to move on to the next.

4. At the beginning of each session, check in with the individuals in your class regarding their experience with their home practice. If they do not feel comfortable with the stage that they have been practicing, review the stage with them, address any problems or questions they still have, and then encourage them to continue practicing it until they are ready to move on to the next stage. If you are not under time constraints and you sense that your class needs more practice on a particular stage, do a class practice on that stage and postpone teaching the next stage.

5. You can read and/or memorize the appropriate text from chapter 7 in the workbook to teach the five stages of Applied Relaxation Training. You can instruct your students to do the same for their home practice.

6. *Optional:* You can make an audiotape of the relaxation exercises in each of the five stages of Applied Relaxation Training based on the text in the workbook. You can use this tape in teaching the five relaxation exercises to your students. You can recommend that your students make their own home practice tape based on the text in the workbook.

7. *Optional:* Use the audiotape *Applied Relaxation Training* published by New Harbinger Publications to teach the stages. Recommend to your students that they purchase their own copies of this tape for home practice.

Stage 1: Progressive Relaxation

1. Use the Basic Procedure on pages 32 and 33 in the workbook. Also see page 63 in the workbook.

2. Have your students do two 15-minute home practices a day.

3. Remind your students that their goal is to relax their entire body in one 15-minute session.

Stage 2: Release-Only Relaxation

1. Use the text on pages 63 and 64 in the workbook.

2. Note that Release-Only Relaxation is a gentler exercise than Progressive Relaxation. For people with injuries or extremely tense individuals who report that Progressive Relaxation is painful for them, suggest that they start with Release-Only Relaxation. They can then return to the more active tensing of Progressive Relaxation when they are more relaxed, or skip it.

Stage 3: Cue-Controlled Relaxation

1. Use the text on pages 64 and 65 in the workbook.

2. Have your students continue their twice-a-day daily practice. Suggest that they rate how relaxed they become, using the 10-point scale on page 19 of the workbook. Tell them that they will be ready to move on to the next stage when they can relax their entire body using cue-controlled relaxation in two to three minutes.

Stage 4: Rapid Relaxation

1. Use the text on pages 65 and 66 in the workbook.

2. Underscore that this stage is to create the habit of checking in with oneself many times a day, noting any symptoms of anxiety or tension, then relaxing deeply.

3. The goal of this stage is to relax in 30 seconds in natural and nonstressful situations. Save the stressful situations for Stage 5.

Stage 5: Applied Relaxation

1. Give some examples of the body's early warning signs of stress and then ask your students for examples of their early warning signs.

2. Take your students through the three-step exercise on pages 66 and 67 after they have jogged in place vigorously. Invite questions and comments.

3. Take them through the same exercise after they imagine a stressful situation and start to get in touch with their distressing feelings. Invite questions and comments.

4. Describe how to use Applied Relaxation in a real-life stressful situation. Ask for examples of situations in which individuals can practice Applied Relaxation in the next week. Invite questions and comments.

Special Considerations

1. See page 67 in the workbook.

2. Encourage your students to create the habit of scanning their body for tension and practicing the rapid relaxation technique at least once a day.

3. *Note:* The authors deleted one of the stages of Applied Relaxation, known as Differential Relaxation, to save time. In their clinical practice they found that Applied Relaxation was effective without it.

8

Self-Hypnosis

Introduction

Purpose: Self-hypnosis can be used as a form of deep relaxation, using positive suggestions to enhance stress management and personal goals.

Time: 10 minutes

Instructions:

1. Give about a five-minute introductory lecture based on pages 69 to 70 in the workbook and then invite questions to further clarify what hypnosis is and is not, and what hypnosis can and cannot do.

2. Invite people to briefly describe their experiences and concerns with hypnosis. You can use the positive descriptions to underscore the many ways that hypnosis can be applied. You can use negative descriptions to clarify and allay fears and reservations regarding experiencing hypnosis now.

The Power of Suggestion

Purpose: These are simple exercises that demonstrate to the novice that the subconscious mind, responding to simple suggestions, can take over automatic muscle movement and allow the individual to respond without conscious effort.

Time: Each of these exercises takes no more than 5 minutes.

Space: Have your students stand at least an arm's length apart.

Instructions:

1. See page 71 of the workbook.

2. Have your students stand, then take them through these two exercises.

The Self-Induction

Purpose: The best way to introduce your students to hypnotic induction is through a demonstration in which they experience a light to medium trance.

Time: 30 minutes

Instructions:

1. Briefly describe the various elements of a self-hypnotic induction (see Personalized Self-Induction on pages 71 to 73 in the workbook).

2. Before starting the induction, have your students select a word or phrase such as "relax now" or "peaceful, safe, and warm" or anything else that has a pleasant and relaxing connotation; for example, their favorite color or place. Tell participants that they will have an opportunity to use this key word or phrase during the induction.

3. Read the Basic Self-Induction Script on pages 73 to 74 in the workbook, or play the 15-minute induction on side 1 of the audiotape *Self-Hypnosis*, published by New Harbinger Publications.

4. When you have completed the induction, return to your normal voice.

5. Suggest that participants get up and stretch. Give people ample time to come out of their trance. You may want to call a five-minute break, and encourage people to get up and walk around.

6. With a large group, have people break into groups of four to discuss their experience with this exercise. Get them thinking about how they can improve your induction to fit their particular needs. Have them share what was most and least compelling about the induction for them. Have them ask any questions that come to mind. Have one person from each group report any interesting comments or unanswered questions to the large group. With a small group, have each person share in turn.

7. After you have dealt with any unanswered questions, go over the key rules for a successful self-induction (see page 73 of the workbook).

Abbreviated Inductions and Five-Finger Exercise

Purpose: These are mini-relaxation exercises that create feelings of calm and alertness. The Five-Finger Exercise is useful for people who have low energy, are depressed, or are suffering from low self-esteem.

Time: These inductions take less than five minutes to teach, and only moments to perform once a person becomes proficient with self-hypnosis.

Instructions: The shorthand techniques, such as the "pencil drop" described on page 75, are optional.

Hypnotic Suggestions

Purpose: Many symptoms of stress are a result of learned habitual responses to stress. Once in a relaxed state of mind, a person is more suggestible. This is an opportunity to suggest new ways of responding to old stresses.

Time: 15 to 30 minutes

Instructions:

1. Go over the rules for hypnotic suggestions on pages 76 and 77 of the workbook. Then have your students write hypnotic suggestions for the 14 problems listed on page 77 of the workbook.

2. Have them compare their answers with those in the workbook on pages 77 to 79.

3. Have them write down at least three of their own problems and then write hypnotic suggestions for each one of them.

4. *Optional:* If you do not have time to do this exercise in class, you can suggest that your students do it as homework.

5. Whether this exercise is a class or homework assignment, you will need to give your students an opportunity to correct their errors on the hypnotic suggestions applied to their own problems. This can be done in groups of four, followed by the reporter from each group bringing up comments or questions when all groups come together. If your group is small, have each person share in turn.

6. *Optional:* You can go over the first several problems in the workbook with the class as a whole. Ask for hypnotic suggestions from class members for each of the problems. Quickly shift to asking for real problems from the class. Ask for hypnotic suggestions for each of these problems. With this option, you are able to immediately explain errors, and to give some additional good examples.

7. Suggest as homework that your students write and audiotape their own self-induction, and to include one or more of the hypnotic suggestions dealing with problems they want to work on. Tell them to listen to this tape once a day for a week, and report back on their experience.

Self-Hypnotic Induction for a Specific Problem

Purpose: This optional exercise on pages 79 to 81 of the workbook outlines how to use self-hypnosis as part of a general plan to resolve a particular problem. The specific problem used in the example is insomnia.

Time: 5 minutes to 1 hour and 50 minutes

Instructions (Options):

1. Give a brief lecture, using the example in the workbook, to explain how an individual needs to analyze her problem, define her goal, change external factors if she can, and work on irrational and stressful thoughts before she is ready to create positive auto-suggestions and a self-induction (5 minutes).

2. Follow Option 1 with the Basic Self-Induction Script with the Sleep Induction (20 minutes).

3. Follow Option 1 with an exercise in which each individual selects a problem to work on and writes out the answers to the following questions at home or in class. Invite questions in the large group or have your students break into dyads to review each other's answers to questions A through G so that they can give each other constructive feedback on questions B, E, D, and G (50 minutes).

    A. What is your specific problem?

    B. What is your goal?

    C. What external factors are contributing to your problem?

    D. What can you do to eliminate or change each one of these external factors so that they no longer contribute to your problem?

    E. What positive suggestions can you create for your induction that take into account each one of these external factors?

    F. What are you saying to yourself that is irrational, distressing, and/or nonproductive that contributes to your problem?

    G. What positive suggestions can you create for your induction that take into account each one of these negative thoughts?

4. After your students have completed Option 3, give them the homework assignment to write an induction tailored to their particular problem, incorporating their goals and other positive auto suggestions. Recommend that they review the sections of the workbook on Personalized Self-Induction, Basic Self-Induction Script, and Hypnotic Suggestions. Have them slowly read their induction in a monotonous tone of voice into a tape recorder and then play it back to themselves so they can experience it. If they do not have access to a recorder, they can have someone else read it to them. If they like, they can further refine their induction by building in more of the suggestions that they find most effective and eliminating the ones that are least effective (5 minutes).

5. Following Option 3, have your students write out their positive auto suggestions about their goal and so forth in the order in which they would like to hear them in an induction. Show your students where they can insert their positive auto suggestions into the Basic Self-Induction at the point designated for posthypnotic suggestion on page 74 in the workbook (5 to 10 minutes).

6. Following Option 5, have your students read their induction into a tape recorder and then listen to it, or have someone read it to them for homework. Remind them to speak in a slow, monotonous tone of voice and repeat each suggestion at least three times (2 minutes).

7. Following Option 5, have your students break into dyads. Have one person slowly read in a monotone the Basic Self-Induction Script plus the other person's list of positive auto suggestions as the other person experiences the trance. Remind the reader to repeat each suggestion at least three times. Have the person who experienced the trance consider which suggestions worked best for him and which he would want to change. Reverse roles, and repeat (45 minutes).

Special Considerations

These points on pages 81 and 82 can be made at the conclusion of your presentation on self-hypnosis or addressed as they come up during the presentation. Be absolutely sure that you cover the first point involving safety!

Audiotape

The New Harbinger Publications cassette tape *Self-Hypnosis* covers all the major points in the workbook chapter. Most important, it includes two inductions that demonstrate the nonverbal aspects of self-hypnosis such as tone of voice, cadence, and pauses.

Side 1, which is 27 minutes long, includes:

- Introduction to Self-Hypnosis

- Exercises on Postural Sway and Postural Suggestion to demonstrate the power of suggestion

- 15-minute induction

- Five rules on how to do effective inductions

Side 2, which is 30 minutes, includes:

- Four ways to deepen an induction

- Ten-minute induction, incorporating the four deepening techniques

- Abbreviated inductions

- How to create and use hypnotic suggestions

9

Autogenics

Introduction

Purpose: Autogenic training is a systematic method of relaxation, using auto suggestion.

Time: 30 minutes

Materials: For students without a workbook, a list of autogenic phrases.

Instructions:

1. See pages 83 through 90 of the workbook.

2. Give a brief historical introduction to Autogenics.

3. Explain briefly the physiology of each of the basic six verbal formulas for physical regulation.

4. State the contraindications as well as the benefits.

5. Explain and give examples of:

   - The three basic Autogenic Training (AT) postures

   - Settling into a position that is comfortable for you

   - Passive concentration

   - Silent, steady repetition of the verbal formula

   - Use of visual, auditory, and tactile images to enhance the verbal formula (e.g., arms made of lead, warm sun, steady metronome, or child's swing)

   - Returning to the formula when distracted

- Autogenic discharges

- Ending an AT session with "When I open my eyes I will feel refreshed and alert"

Make sure your students are not still in a trancelike state as they move on to their regular activities.

6. Slowly read the five sets of Autogenic Formulas for Normalizing the Body on pages 87 and 88 in the workbook. Be sure to properly pace yourself. Intersperse Autogenic Formulas for Calming the Mind such as "I am calm and relaxed" every other line or so.

7. Instruct your students to say to themselves the first line four times, taking five seconds each time and pausing three seconds between each recitation. Have them do the same for each of the lines. Demonstrate the pace, as the class practices.

8. If they do not have their own workbook, give your students a typed version to refer to as they go through the formulas on their own.

9. In a small group, invite each student to talk about her experience. In a large group, have one person from each of the small groups summarize comments or questions.

10. Suggest that they practice this brief version at home at least twice a day for a week.

11. Once the students have mastered the basic six verbal formulas for physical regulation, they are ready to try the Autogenic Modification Exercises briefly described in the workbook on page 89.

12. Cover the items under Special Consideration on pages 89 and 90 in the workbook that are relevant to your group.

Audiotape

The New Harbinger Publications cassette tape *Autogenics* is 37 minutes long and goes through the 12-week program described in the workbook.

10

Brief Combination Techniques

Introduction

Purpose: Therapists have found that many of the techniques already presented have a more profound effect when combined.

Instructions:

1. See pages 91 through 97 in the workbook.

Special Notes

While all these exercises can be used for relaxation, the following are a few suggestions as to other purposes they can serve.

- Exercises for quick relaxation:

    1. Stretch and Relax

    2. Autogenic Breathing

- Exercises for thought stopping:

    3. Stop and Breathe

    4. Changing Channels

- Exercises to enhance self-esteem and mood:

    5. I Am Grateful

    8. Breath Counting

    10. Accepting Yourself

- Exercises to reduce pain and tension:

  7. The Tension Cutter

- Exercises to enhance sense of self-control:

  6. Deep Affirmation

  9. Taking Control

11

Recording Your Own
Relaxation Tape

Introduction

Purpose: To explain and demonstrate how students can make relaxation tapes tailored to their own particular needs.

Time: 20 to 40 minutes

Instructions:

1. See pages 99 to 105 in the workbook.

2. This is an optional topic.

3. Demonstrate how you record your voice as you take your students through a relaxation exercise. You may choose to use part of the Relaxation Script on pages 101 to 104 in the workbook. At the end of the relaxation exercise, be sure to suggest that when they open their eyes and return to the room they will feel relaxed, refreshed, and alert. When they open their eyes, encourage them to stretch and move around. Call for questions and comments. You may want to schedule a short break.

4. Play back a brief section of what you recorded. Ask class members what they think are the ingredients of a good relaxation audiotape. Follow this discussion with any additional suggestions that have not been covered.

12

Refuting Irrational Ideas

Introduction

Purpose: Rational Emotive Therapy (RET) reduces stressful emotions and physiological arousal by identifying a person's irrational, extremely negative self-talk and changing it to rational, appropriate, and less extreme self-talk.

Time: 1 hour

Materials: At least one copy of the homework sheet on page 123 in the workbook for each student. They can make additional copies from their workbook or from the copy that you give them.

Instructions:

1. Briefly describe the basic tenets of RET as outlined on workbook pages 107 to 109.

2. Some people take an hour or more to fill out and score the Belief Inventory on pages 110 to 115 of the workbook. If your time is limited, have your students do it as homework or skip it.

3. You will need this time to give a lecture including at least the first 10 of the 21 irrational ideas. Explain why they are irrational and extreme, and give examples of less extreme and more appropriate ideas for each irrational idea (see pages 115 to 119 in the workbook).

4. Conclude this lecture with the Rules to Promote Rational Thinking on page 119 of the workbook and then answer any questions.

5. Walk your students through steps A through E for Refuting Irrational Ideas in the workbook on pages 119 to 121. Go over the homework example. Then call for an example from students and take the class through steps A through E again.

6. Give class members the homework assignment to spend at least 20 minutes a day doing this exercise, using examples from their daily lives. Suggest that they make copies of the blank homework sheet to fill in for their convenience.

7. At the beginning of the following session, have the students go over their homework in groups of four. Have them each share one example of steps A through E and get corrective feedback from their particular group. Then have one member of the group report back to the large group any interesting comments or questions. If you have a small group, have each student share in turn.

8. After you deal with unanswered questions in the large group, you may want to review the special considerations on page 121 of the workbook.

9. Tell your students to get into the habit of asking themselves, "What am I feeling?" and "What am I telling myself about this situation?" whenever they have an extremely negative emotional response to a situation. In this way, they will learn to identify their irrational self-talk, have an opportunity to mentally go through this homework assignment, and learn to tell themselves something less extreme and more appropriate that will generate less stressful emotions.

Rational Emotive Imagery

Purpose: Use imagination to change excessively unpleasant emotional responses to stressful events into less intense, more appropriate emotional responses.

Time: 30 minutes

This technique is not as complicated and time-consuming to teach as Refuting Irrational Ideas. If you are pressed for time and can teach only one of the cognitive techniques, you may prefer to try this one.

Instructions:

1. Briefly go over the five steps for Rational Emotive Imagery with the class, using an example. See pages 124 to 126 of the workbook.

2. Have the class take a few minutes to get into a comfortable position and relax.

3. Take students one step at a time through the five steps again, instructing them to focus on a stressful event of their own. Give them ample time to use their imagination to transform their original response to their stressful situation into a more appropriate one.

4. When they are through, have them write down their original emotions, their new emotions, and what they changed in their belief system in order to get from one to the other.

5. Have participants share their experiences in groups of three or four. The people in the small group can offer suggestions for alternative beliefs to assist an individual who

had difficulty shifting from the more extreme to the less extreme emotions. Have one person report back to the large group with any unanswered questions.

6. Go over the three levels of insight necessary to change habitual emotional responses. These insight levels are listed at the top of page 126 of the workbook.

7. As a homework assignment, you can suggest that your students practice Rational Emotive Imagery 10 minutes a day for a week. On page 125 of the workbook is a list of sample situations and alternative emotional responses. You can ask your students to fill in their own stressful situations, along with their stressful and more appropriate emotions, on page 125. They can use this list to practice Rational Emotive Imagery.

13

Thought Stopping

Introduction

Purpose: This chapter presents two basic methods of thought stopping aimed at eliminating nonproductive, distressing cognitions.

Time: 15 to 30 minutes

Materials: A timer with an alarm, rubber bands (optional)

Instructions:

1. Clarify the difference between useful worry and nonproductive worry. You can do this by either posing the question to the group or giving a brief explanation. Then have the group offer examples of useful worry and nonproductive worry. See the first half of page 128 in the workbook to help fuel this discussion.

2. Briefly describe this technique: its purpose and origin and the various explanations for its success (see page 127 of the workbook).

3. For step 1, instruct the individuals in your group to write down several of their stressful cognitions. Follow the instructions in the workbook on page 129. If your group members do not have their own workbook, write the questions listed in this step on the board so that they can refer to them when they evaluate their thoughts. If you are pressed for time, read aloud the questions listed in this step and have the individuals in your group each think of a distressing, irrational, useless thought that they want to get rid of.

4. Follow steps 2 to 4, described on pages 129 and 130 of the workbook. Steps 2 and 3 can be combined in the first practice of a "startler" technique that includes saying loudly, "Stop!" at the sound of the buzzer (or when you, the leader, shout "stop."). Once step 3

is mastered, in subsequent practices the members of your group can proceed to step 4 and practice saying "Stop!" progressively more softly on their own without a timer. Finally, instruct them to imagine hearing "Stop!" shouted.

5. Before practicing for step 5, be sure that everyone has one or more positive assertive cognitions to substitute for their old distressing cognition. Give or solicit a few examples of distressing cognitions. For each of these, come up with an appropriate positive substitute thought. Instruct the individuals in the group to write a couple of substitute thoughts that they can refer to should the first one become less effective through repetition. Now they are ready to imagine their distressing thought as they did in step 2 and then choose when to shift to one of their positive, assertive substitute thoughts (typically in one to three minutes).

6. Emphasize that to succeed with Thought Stopping, it must be practiced daily. Intentionally bringing to mind the distressing thought and then stopping it with the startler technique or thought substitution gives you greater awareness and more control over your negative cognition. When you are fairly consistently successful with this, you are ready to use your preferred version of the thought stopping technique anytime the negative cognition comes into your awareness.

7. Suggest other types of thought substitution that work well:

   • A pleasant fantasy or memory completely unrelated to the stressful thought.

   • An activity such as whistling or singing, or getting up and walking around.

Thought substitution can be described as "changing the radio station when you don't like what you are listening to."

8. Review the special considerations on pages 130 and 131 of the workbook with your students.

9. Tell them to work on only one stressful thought at a time. It is important that they make an agreement with themselves at the onset to use thought stopping every time they catch themselves having the stressful thought.

10. Point out to your students that by following the instructions, a stressful thought can be neutralized within a few days. This does not mean that a person will never have the stressful thought again. But it does seem to lose its power and occur much less frequently. Occasionally, a person will have to use Thought Stopping more than once on an old stressful thought that reappears.

Audiotape

The New Harbinger cassette tape *Thought Stopping* is 20 minutes long. It explains the technique and goes through the steps in the workbook. It even has varying timed intervals of silence for dwelling on the stressful thought and signals when to stop.

Eye Movement Technique Instructions

Purpose: This technique is helpful in managing or controlling anxiety associated with recent or past events. Once mastered, EMT can be applied to all types of stress, varying from event-specific events to chronic anxiety.

Time: 30 minutes

Instructions:

1. See pages 131 to 133 in the workbook.

2. Have the individuals in your group close their eyes and think of a event in their recent or remote past that causes them distress when they dwell on it and about which they would like to feel more at peace. Tell them to choose an event that causes "unpleasant discomfort" (a 5 to 6 on a scale of 0 to 10) and not extreme fear.

3. Suggest that if their distress level is lower than 5, they can imagine specific details and dwell on the "what ifs" or "oh no's!" associated with the stressful event until their stress level is at 5 or 6. If their stress level is higher than 6, instruct them to pick another distressing event with a distress level of 5 or 6 for the purpose of this practice. Remind them not to proceed with EMT until their stress level is 5 or 6. Have them raise their hands when they have in mind a distressing event with a discomfort level of 5 or 6.

4. You can proceed with steps 3 through 5 in the workbook when everyone in your group has distressing cognitions for which they feel "unpleasant discomfort." Repeat steps 3 through 5 at least three times.

5. Have the members of your group practice EMT on their own at home.

6. Usually by the end of three repetitions of EMT, individuals will note a reduction in distress regarding their negative event. If extreme levels of stress continue to be associated with the event even after a couple of home practices, suggest that they consider seeing a licensed therapist, particularly one with training in Eye Movement Desensitization and Reprocessing.

14

Worry Control

Introduction

Purpose: People fuel their anxiety by anticipating unlikely stressful events and engaging in activities to prevent these events. This chapter offers several methods to manage your worry: problem solving, relaxation, risk assessment, scheduling worry time, worry exposure, and worry-behavior prevention.

Time: Four to six weeks, including weeks of home practice between instructional sessions 1 hour and 30 minutes to 2 hours each.

Materials: chart pad and/or board, paper and writing implements

Distinguishing Healthy Versus Unhealthy Worry

Time: 15 minutes

Instructions:

Lead a discussion about worry, asking questions such as:

- What is worry?

- What are some examples of things you worry about a lot?

- When does worry become a serious problem and therefore might be considered unhealthy?

- When is worrying healthy or useful?

Keep in mind that people who need to learn this material often initially feel anxious about revealing their worries and have difficulty with concentration. Therefore it's good to warm up the group to this topic by writing on a chart pad or board their examples of worry.

You may want to save this list to use to illustrate the exercises covered in this chapter. With a little coaxing, and perhaps a couple of your own examples, most groups can generate a list of at least ten worries in a short time. Next, write two headings on the board or chart pad—"Healthy Worry" and "Unhealthy Worry"—and then fill in the characteristics of each, as the group answers your questions. See pages 135 to 137 in the workbook for ideas on this topic.

Worry into Problem Solving

Time: 30 minutes

Instructions:

1. See pages 137 to 139 in the workbook.

2. Go over the steps of problem solving either using the example in the workbook or an example volunteered by a member of the group.

3. Make extra copies of the Problem-Solving Worksheet. Have the individuals in your group fill out the worksheet in class or as homework. It should take about 15 minutes.

4. Have the group break into dyads and share their Problem-Solving Worksheets for about 5 minutes. Encourage the listeners to give feedback.

5. Back in the large group, discuss questions and comments.

Four Steps to Managing Your Worry

Instructions:

1. Briefly introduce the four steps.

2. See pages 139 to 149 in the workbook.

Step 1: Relaxation.

If the members of your group have already mastered Applied Relaxation described in chapter 7 of the workbook, you can skip this step. Otherwise, teach one step a week, giving them an opportunity to practice twice daily between sessions.

Optional: The appropriate sections of the audiotape *Applied Relaxation Training*, listed at the end of chapter 7 in the workbook may be used for group practice and/or home practice.

Step 2: Risk Assessment (1 hour)

A. If you haven't already, take a few minutes to ask for examples of typical chronic worries and list them on the board or chart pad.

B. Go over the three basic cognitive distortions of chronic worriers. Chronic worriers tend to:

1. Focus on the worst *possible* consequence no matter how unlikely it is to occur; the less terrible yet more *probable* outcomes are largely ignored.

2. *Magnify* their images of the *worst case outcome* into catastrophic disaster.

3. *Minimize their capacity to cope* with negative outcomes.

C. Identify the distortions in the examples of chronic worry on the board.

D. Explain how to fill out the Risk Assessment Form, using the example on pages 140 and 141 in the workbook.

E. Instruct the individuals in your group to fill out a blank copy of the Risk Assessment Form on their own. See pages 142 to 143 in the workbook. It is best that this be done during group time, as anxious people sometimes have difficulty writing down their worries and will need your encouragement and supervision. This should take 15 to 20 minutes.

F. Have the individuals go over their completed Risk Assessment Forms in dyads. Encourage the listeners to give feedback. This should take about five to ten minutes.

G. Discuss any remaining questions and comments when the large group reconvenes.

H. Hand out a blank Risk Assessment Form for home practice. Tell your group members to make several copies of this form and practice using the form on several of their worries during the next week.

I. Go over their home practice at the beginning of your next group session in dyads or in the larger group.

Step 3: Scheduling Worry Time and Worry Exposure (1 hour)

Scheduling Worry Time. Refer to page 144 in the workbook. When you instruct your group about scheduling worry time as home practice, suggest that they may want to pick a "worry chair" to sit in, and to buy a "worry notebook" to write out their worries. Encourage them to schedule daily worry appointments for at least one week. Go over their home practice at the beginning of your next group session. What was their experience like? What did they learn?

Worry Exposure

A. Briefly explain the instructions for Worry Exposure, referring to pages 144 to 146 in the workbook

B. If you are pressed for time, have the individuals in your group do the first two instructions of Worry Exposure at home, preferably after several days of practice with Scheduling Worry Time.

C. Lead your group through instructions 3 through 7 of Worry Exposure.

D. Discuss their questions and comments.

E. Instruct your group to practice instruction 8 of Worry Exposure during their scheduled worry time daily for the next week.

F. Review the home practice at the beginning of your next group session. In dyads or in the larger group, allow each individual to describe his or her experience with Worry Exposure. Troubleshoot why some individuals did not practice Worry Exposure and encourage them to try it over the next week.

Step 4. Worry-Behavior Prevention (45 minutes)

A. Explain how worry behavior perpetuates anxiety, referring to page 146 of the workbook. Give several examples. Invite members of the group to give examples of their own. Write these examples on the board or chart pad.

B. Lead your group through instructions 1 to 3 of Worry-Behavior Prevention, referring to pages 146 to 148 in the workbook. After you have explained one of the three instructions and given an example of it from the workbook, pause while the individuals in your group write down their response. Encourage individuals to share their examples and discuss questions before going on to the next step of Worry-Behavior Prevention.

C. Tell your group to practice instructions 3 through 5 of Worry-Behavior Prevention over the next week. Urge them to write down what happens when they do instruction 4 of Worry-Behavior Prevention. This is particularly important in order to confront their fears with the facts.

D. Review the home practice at the beginning of your next group session. Allow 10 to 15 minutes for individuals to discuss their experience in dyads or in the larger group. Troubleshoot why some individuals did not practice Worry-Behavior Prevention and encourage them to try it over the next week.

Review and Relapse Prevention

Time: 15 minutes

Instructions:

A. Briefly review the skills that you taught from this chapter with your group.

B. Remind them that anxiety and worry are inevitable and natural and sometimes even helpful. Tell them that anxious worriers tend to be intelligent, sensitive, and imaginative people who can use their ample abilities to confront their worries that are not helpful.

C. Ask which skills they found the most useful and why.

D. Ask for specific examples of when they are likely to need these skills in the future.

E. Encourage them to practice these skills regularly.

F. Suggest that the next time they worry would be a good opportunity to practice one or more of these skills.

15

Coping Skills Training

Introduction

Purpose: This chapter is divided into two parts: coping skills training for anxiety and coping skills training for anger. Use coping skills to diminsh anticipatory anxiety and to manage distressing emotions and irrational thoughts when faced with stressful situations. Coping Skills Training is the one technique in this book that deals with managing anger.

Time: Ideally this technique should be taught over a minimum of four 60 to 90 minutes group training sessions, with each session followed by a week of home practice.

Material: paper and pencil

Coping Skills Training for Anxiety

Introduction (15 minutes)

A. Briefly go over the concept that it is the interpretation of the event and not the event itself that creates stressful emotions, referring to pages 151 and 152 in the workbook.

B. Particularly if you have not covered chapter 12 in the workbook, *Refuting Irrational Ideas*, reinforce this concept with a brief guided fantasy such as the following: "Imagine your boss (or authority figure in your life if you are not working) walking into your work area, stopping and staring at you for a moment without saying a word, and then leaving. What are your thoughts about this? What are your feelings?" Go around the group and ask for each person's response. Point out that the same stimulus generated a variety of interpretations. Depending on the interpretation, the emotions also varied.

C. Explain the purpose of Coping Skills Training (see the top of page 152 in the workbook).

D. Briefly describe the five steps of Coping Skills Training (see page 152 in the workbook).

Step 1: Learn to Relax Efficiently (15 to 30 minutes)

A. If the individuals in your group are not familiar with the relaxation exercises recommended for this technique on page 153 in the workbook, teach one exercise a week, giving them an opportunity to practice the exercise twice a day for a week. To save time, teach diaphragmatic breathing or relaxation without tension followed by special-place visualization in the same session.

Step 2: Make a Stressful-Events Hierarchy (45 to 60 minutes)

A. After you have explained the purpose of a hierarchy and how to construct one (see pages 153 through 155 in the workbook), have the members of your group begin to construct a hierarchy of their own.

B. If there is not time to finish the hierarchies during group time, they can be finished at home.

C. Review the hierarchies in dyads or in the large group. Make sure that the hierarchies are about behaviors that are convenient to do (for example, drive on a freeway) and/or that the individual is willing to expend resources to do them (for example, fly on a plane).

Step 3: Create Stress-Coping Thoughts (1 hour)

A. Explain the purpose of stress-coping thoughts and how they work, using the example on pages 155 and 156.

B. List the four times to use stress-coping thoughts, along with examples of generic stress-coping thoughts for each of these times, listed on pages 156 and 157 of the workbook.

C. Explain and illustrate how to create your own stress-coping thoughts, using one or more of the examples in the workbook on pages 158 to 159.

D. Lead the members of your group through the steps to create two or three of their own stress-coping thoughts that they can use to counter their anxious thoughts and relax their bodies when faced with one of the stressful situations they listed on their hierarchy. Refer to pages 158 to160 in the workbook.

E. Instruct the individuals in your group to create two or three of their own stress-coping thoughts in a similar manner for each of the stressful situations listed on their hierarchy as homework. If they can't think of their own stress-coping thoughts, they can choose from the general list of stress-coping thoughts on pages 156 and 157. If the members of your group do not have a copy of the workbook, make extra copies of pages 156 through 160 for them to use as a guide when doing their homework.

F. Review homework at the beginning of the next session.

Step 4: Imago Coping Skills for Anxiety (1 hour)

A. Begin by briefly explaining this step, outlining 4A through E on the board (see pages 160 and 161 in the workbook).

B. Have the members of your group review the first scene on their stressful-events hierarchy along with their stress-coping thoughts for that scene.

C. Proceed with 4A and B on pages 160 and 161 in the workbook. It usually takes a minute or two for most people to imagine their scene with enough detail to become anxious. Have the members of your group raise their hands when they have their scene in mind and are feeling anxious because of it. When everyone in the group has raised their hands, give the instructions for 4C in the workbook. In another minute, instruct your group to rate their anxiety on a scale from 0 to 10. Finally, tell your group to relax in their special place and use cue- controlled relaxation.

D. Call for comments and questions. If some individuals had difficulty sensing their stressful scene and thus felt no anxiety, suggest ways to intensify their imagery, remind them to imagine themselves in the scene, and encourage them to catastrophize. These people should repeat the first scene to see if they can raise their anxiety levels above level 3. For people who experience no reduction in anxiety when using their coping statements, assist them in replacing their coping statements with new ones. See Special Considerations in the workbook on page 173 to address other common problems.

E. Before repeating 4B through E in the workbook, instruct people in your group whose anxiety levels were 1 or 0 after using their coping skills to go on to the next scene on their stressful-event hierarchy and to review their coping statements for this new scene. For those whose anxiety levels remained 2 or higher, tell them to imagine the same scene again in vivid detail. Instruct your group to relax in their special place and use cue-controlled relaxation; then take them through 4B to E in the workbook for the second time.

F. Repeat 4B through E in the workbook again for a total of at least three times, pausing between each round to assist with problems.

G. Encourage the members of your group to practice Imago Coping Skills at home on a daily basis for at least 15 minutes.

H. Follow up in the next session on your group's experience with Imago Coping Skills.

Step 5: In Vivo Coping Skills (1 hour)

A. Explain how to do step 5, using the example in the workbook on pages 162 and 163.

B. Ask the members of your group to pick a scene from their stressful-events hierarchy that they can do in real life in the next week. Ideally they will work from the low anxiety-provoking scenes on their hierarchy to the high anxiety-provoking scenes, but they may be more motivated to work on something that they have to do or have been putting off.

C. Have them write down stress-coping thoughts for their scene that they can use for: 1. Preparation; 2. Confronting; 3. Coping with fear; and 4. Reinforcing success. Encourage them to think about where they can put these stress-coping thoughts so that they will be easily accessible when they need them. Have them review their scene and stress-coping thoughts in dyads.

D. Instruct your group to practice their In Vivo Coping Skills for their scene as homework. Suggest that while using coping skills in real life at first may seem awkward, with practice it will become almost automatic. If they forget to use their coping skills, they can practice them in their imaginations as they did in step 4 and commit to using their coping skills the next time they have an opportunity in real life. Encourage them to begin using their coping skills at the first sign of tension in real life.

E. Follow up in the next session on your group's experience with In Vivo Coping Skills.

Coping Skills Training for Anger

Introduction (15 minutes)

A. See the introduction to Coping Skills Training for Anxiety at the beginning of this chapter.

B. Briefly describe the two types of thoughts that lead to anger and the fight or flight response (see page 163 in the workbook).

Step 1: Learn to Relax Efficiently (15 to 30 minutes)

A. Explain how the fight or flight response is an important component of anger, using the example on pages 163 and 164 of the workbook.

B. If the individuals in your group are not familiar with the relaxation exercises recommended for this technique on page 153 in the workbook, teach one exercise a week, giving them an opportunity to practice the exercise twice a day for a week.

Step 2: Make a Stressful-Events Hierarchy (1 hour)

A. After you have explained the purpose of a hierarchy and demonstrated how to construct one (see pages 164 and 165 in the workbook), have the members of your group begin to construct a hierarchy of their own.

B. If there is not time to finish the hierarchies during group time, they can be finished at home.

C. Review the hierarchies in dyads or the large group.

Step 3: Create Stress-Coping Thoughts for Anger (1 hour to 1 hour and 30 minutes)

A. Present the material for this step in a manner that is appropriate for your audience. Possible options include one or a combination of the following:

1. Assign pages 166 through 169 in the workbook as homework and follow this up with a class discussion covering the major points.

2. Didactic presentation of the material on these pages.

3. Begin a class discussion on this topic with a role play of two people having an argument or simply one person recounting how he or she has been wronged by another. Using the Socratic method, ask questions of the group to pull out the major points of this section. For example: "Sounds as though Tom assumes that Susie has violated an important rule and therefore she is wrong and bad, and he has a right to be mad. What are a couple of problems with this assumption?" Follow up this discussion with a question such as, "What could Tom say to himself that would counter his "should" statements and blaming statements and allow him to deal with Susie's behavior without getting so angry and stressed out?"

B. Explain how to create your own stress-coping thoughts using the questions and example on pages 170 to 171 in the workbook.

C. Lead your group through a guided imagery exercise in which they visualize the first scene on their stressful-events hierarchy. Use the questions on the top of page 170 to help the individuals in your group identify their angry thoughts. Then instruct your group to use what they have learned about blaming statements, "should" statements, and personal responsibility to counter their angry thoughts with stress-coping thoughts.

D. On the board or chart pad, duplicate the four-column chart on the bottom of page 169 in the workbook, giving ample room for stressful thoughts and stress-coping thoughts. Ask for an example from the group based on their experience with the guided imagery exercise and fill it in on the four-column chart. Have the individuals in your group copy the four-column chart from the board and fill in their example from the guided imagery exercise. Address questions and comments.

E. Give the group another 5 to 10 minutes to imagine on their own the next scene on their stressful-events hierarchy, identify their anger-provoking thoughts, and come up with stress-coping thoughts. Have them go over their two examples in dyads.

F. Assign as homework writing down their stressful thoughts and stress-coping thoughts for each of these scenes on their stressful-events hierarchy. In the next session, review homework in dyads or in the large group.

Step 4: Imago Coping Skills for Anger (1 hour)

A. Explain how to do this step, using the example on page 171 in the workbook.

B. Have the members of your group review the first scene on their stressful-events hierarchy along with their stress-coping thoughts for that scene.

C. Proceed with 4A and B on pages 160 and 161 in the workbook, instructing them to focus on the first scene of their stressful hierarchy. Substitute the word "anger" for anxiety, Have the members of your group raise their hands when they have their scene in mind and are feeling at least irritated because of it. On a scale of 0 to 10 for anger, they should feel at least a 3 or a 4. When everyone in the group has raised their hands, give the instructions in 4C in the workbook. In another minute, instruct your group to rate their anger on a scale from 1 to 10. Finally, tell your group to relax in their special place and use cue-controlled relaxation.

D. Call for comments and questions. If some individuals had difficulty sensing their stressful scene and thus felt no anger, suggest ways to intensify their imagery, remind them to imagine themselves in the scene, and suggest they use their "blaming" and "should" statements. These people should repeat the first scene in the next round of practice to see if they can raise their anger levels above level 3. People who experienced no reduction in anger when using their coping statments may just need more practice using them. Check their coping statements. Are they accurate, believable, and calming? If not, suggest alternative, more persuasive coping statements. See Special Considerations in the workbook on page 173 to address other common problems.

E. Before repeating B through E in the workbook, instruct the people in your group who lowered their anger level to a 1 or 0 using coping skills to go on to the next scene on their stressful-event hierarchy. Tell them to review their coping statements for this new scene. For those whose anger levels remained 2 or higher, tell them to imagine the same scene again in vivid detail.

F. Instruct your group to relax in their special place and use cue-controlled relaxation; and then take them through 4B to E in the workbook two more times, pausing between each round to assist with problems.

G. Encourage the individuals in your group to practice this step daily at home for up to 20 minutes. Later they can practice up to 30 minutes daily.

H. In the next group session, spend time in the large group or in dyads discussing their experience practicing this step.

Step 5: In Vivo Coping Skills (1 hour)

A. Explain how to do this step, using the example on pages 172 and 173 of the workbook.

B. Ask the members of your group to pick a scene from their stressful-events hierarchy that they can do in real life in the next week. Ideally they will work from the low anger-provoking scenes on their hierarchy to the high anger-provoking scenes, but they may be more motivated to work on something that they have to do or have been putting off.

C. Have them write down stress-coping thoughts for their scene that they can use for: 1. Preparation; 2. Confronting; 3. Coping with distressing feelings; and 4. Reinforcing success. Encourage them to think about where they can put these stress-coping thoughts so they are easily accessible when they need them.

D. Have them review their scene and stress-coping thoughts in triads. *Optional:* When they have a list of coping statements, have them role-play their scenes with one member of the triad while the other member of the triad serves as a coach.

E. Instruct your group to practice their In Vivo Coping Skills for their scene as homework. Suggest that while using coping skills in real life at first may seem awkward, with practice it will become almost automatic. If they forget to use their coping skills, they can practice them in their imaginations as they did in step 4 and commit to using their coping skills the next time they have an opportunity in real life. Encourage them to begin using their coping skills at the first sign of tension in real life.

F. Follow up in the next session on your group's experience with In Vivo Coping Skills.

16

Goal Setting and Time Management

Introduction

Purpose: The key assumption in this chapter is that to effectively manage your time, you must learn to structure your life around what is most important to you, and to minimize the time you spend on activities that you do not value. Vilfredo Pareto's 80-20 principle is a good way to start thinking about what is most important and what is not.

This chapter teaches you how to clarify your values, define your goals, and develop a plan for reaching them; it invites you to look at how you currently use your time and bring it into closer alignment with your priorities; it gives you tips on how to combat procrastination and more efficiently organize your time.

Time: 5 minutes

Instructions: Give a brief lecture based on pages 175 and 176 in the workbook.

Clarifying Your Values

Time: 30 minutes

Materials: two pieces of paper and a pen for each student

Instructions:

1. See pages 177 to 178 in the workbook.

2. Define values, give some examples of values, and explain why clarifying one's values can be useful.

3. Before you take your class through the guided fantasies, have them clear their laps, get into a comfortable position, close their eyes, and get relaxed. After you have read to them the first scene, give them a few minutes to reflect on it before you have them open their eyes and write their answers. Repeat this process for the second scene. In the large group, or small groups, ask people to share what they learned from this exercise. *Optional questions to ask your students:* Did it confirm what you already knew about yourself? Any surprises? Did your priorities change or stay the same for both scenes?

4. After you have explained the importance of ranking values from the most to least important to them, have your students do it.

5. Invite a discussion by asking questions such as: Does this exercise show you that your priorities mirror how you live your life? Does this exercise help explain why you never seem to get to certain things because you don't value them as much as other things? Does this exercise make you realize that you have been neglecting something that you really value?

Setting Goals

Time: 30 minutes

Materials: one or two pieces of paper and a pen for each student

Instructions:

1. See pages 179 to 182 in the workbook.

2. Define goals and how they differ from values. Explain why it is important for their goals to reflect their values. (5 minutes)

3. Go over the five questions under Designing Effective Goals on page 179 that people should ask themselves. Also go over Balancing Your Goals. Have your students take notes if they do not have the workbook. (5 minutes)

4. Go over the example of how Eric used his list of values to guide him in writing his goals. (5 minutes)

5. Have your students write down at least one goal for each of their values. This is a good homework assignment, or you can give your students at least 15 minutes to work on it in class.

Developing an Action Plan

Time: 1 hour

Materials: one piece of paper (two if they do not have the workbook), a pen, and a blank copy of the Self-Contract for each student

Instructions:

1. See pages 182 to 185 in the workbook.

2. Explain why an Action Plan is so crucial to achieving one's goals. Outline what an effective Action Plan includes. Have your students take notes if they do not have a workbook.

3. Describe the two strategies used to create an Action Plan: *1. Imagine that you have already achieved your goal* and *2. Brainstorming.* Use the examples from the book, or better yet, ask for examples from your audience to illustrate these two strategies.

4. Go over the process of Evaluating Your Progress. Encourage your students to choose a support person with whom they can review their progress. If they don't have one, suggest that they mark on their calendar when they plan to review how they are doing.

5. Explain the Self-Contract. While this may seem corny to some people, research shows that it increases the likelihood of people following through on their goals.

6. Have your students design an Action Plan, using one of the two strategies you have suggested.

7. Have your students write out a Self-Contract based on their Action Plan.

Evaluating How You Spend Your Time

Time: 1 hour class time; 3 days to keep Time Log at home

Materials: one or three blank copies of the Sample Time Log, a blank piece of paper, and a pen for each student

Instructions:

1. See pages 185 to 191 in the workbook.

2. Explain how to keep a Time Log. You can use Samantha's Time Log as an example. If you have the option of having your students keep a Time Log for 3 days and your students are likely to comply, fine. If not, have your students do an estimate of their Time Log.

3. Have your students go over their Time Log, using the system described under Evaluating Your Time Log, and write down the changes they would need to make it more consistent with their values and goals.

4. Invite your students to briefly share (in the large group or in small groups) how they would be willing to change their behavior so that it is more consistent with their values and goals.

Combating Procrastination

Time: 15 minutes

Materials: one piece of paper (two, if they do not have the workbook) and a pen for each student

Instructions:

1. See pages 191 to 193 in the workbook.

2. Have your students write down three situations in which they typically procrastinate. Write a few students' examples on the board.

3. Give a lecture on Combating Procrastination. If your students do not have a copy of the workbook, suggest that they take notes.

4. Have the group suggest ways to combat procrastination in the examples on the board.

5. Have them list a few appropriate suggestions for combating each of the situations in which they typically procrastinate and try them out at home. If possible, be sure to follow up on this home practice assignment at the beginning of the next session.

Organizing Your Time and Organizing Your Day

Time: 20 minutes

Materials: one piece of paper and a pen for each student if they don't have the workbook

Instructions:

1. See pages 193 to 195 in the workbook.

2. This is what most people think the purpose of time management is: by being better organized, one can get more done. This section can be taught independent of the other sections of this chapter. If you are teaching an abbreviated module on time management, it is best to include these two sections.

3. Give a lecture on this topic. If your students do not have a copy of the workbook, recommend that they take notes. Invite questions and comments.

17

Assertiveness Training

Introduction

Purpose: How a person relates to others can be a significant source of stress. Assertive communication allows the individual to set limits and express what he wants, feels, and believes while taking into account the rights and feelings of others. This tends to minimize interpersonal strain.

Mini Assertiveness Course

Time: This is a topic that can easily be expanded into a course all its own. How can you possibly teach Assertiveness Training in an hour or two? If you are pressed for time, here is a suggested outline that you can cover in 1 hour to 1 hour and 30 minutes.

Instructions:

1. *Optional:* Have your students fill in the blanks in response to the six problem situations presented on workbook pages 197 and 199. As they answer these questions, they will become more curious about assertiveness. (5 minutes)

2. Introduce Assertiveness Training (see pages 199 to 200 of the workbook). This may include a list of Mistaken Traditional Assumptions versus Your Legitimate Rights. The list of basic assumptions regarding your rights is optional in this abbreviated presentation because it is so time-consuming (at least 15 minutes). (5 to 8 minutes)

3. Define aggressive, passive, and assertive communication (see page 202 in the workbook). Test your students' ability to distinguish these three styles of interaction by asking them to label the six scenes presented on pages 202 to 204 as aggressive, passive, or assertive. A quick and fun way to do this exercise is to have two people read aloud A's and B's parts in the first scene, ask for the correct label from a student, and

then ask why she chose that particular label. If the label is incorrect, ask if someone else had another label and why she chose that label. Proceed through the other five scenes in this manner. (15 minutes)

4. *Optional:* Have your students go over their answers to the questions on pages 197 to 199 in the workbook and label their responses as aggressive, assertive, or passive. Ask them if their answers tend to fall predominantly under one label. (5 minutes)

5. Instruct your students to fill out the Assertiveness Questionnaire on pages 204 to 207 in the workbook. Discuss in a large group or in dyads their evaluation of their responses. When you are pressed for time, a quick way to get your students to begin to identify areas in which they could be more assertive is to simply ask. If the group is small enough, go around the room and ask each student. Write their answers on the board. If it's a large group, have your students write down their own examples. (You need only write a few of the examples on the board.) Be sure they include the assertive behavior they are not using, the person or type of person they have difficulty with, and when they have difficulty. For example: "Asking for help from my boss when I don't know what to do next." "Saying 'no' to family and friends when I don't want to do something and I don't have other plans."

6. Teach your students the Short Form Assertiveness Technique on pages 214 to 215 of the workbook. Note that this is the same as steps 3, 4, and 5 in Your Script for Change on pages 208 and 209 of the workbook. Demonstrate the Short Form Assertiveness Technique. (10 minutes)

7. Instruct participants to write an assertive message for one of their problem areas. They can refer back to the items they checked off on the Assertiveness Questionnaire to identify a problem area. (5 minutes)

8. In groups of three, have each individual briefly state the "when," the "who," and the "what" of their problem situation and then state their assertive message. The other group members can give constructive feedback about the assertive message. Does it include the three elements: "I think," "I feel," and "I want"? Is it clear? Is it complete? Does it avoid blame? Allow about 5 minutes per group member to present his problem situation and assertive message, and to receive feedback. (15 minutes)

   When you call the large group back together, ask for questions and comments. (5 to 10 minutes)

Long Form

Time: 6 to 8 hours

Instructions:

1. Have your students respond to the six problem situations on pages 197 to 199 of the workbook. You may choose to read the situations and have your students answer on a

blank sheet of paper, make copies of the problem situations available for your students to write on, or have your students answer these questions from their own workbooks at home or in class. (5 minutes)

2. Introduce Assertiveness Training (see pages 199 and the bottom of page 201 of the workbook). (5 minutes)

3. Go over the Mistaken Traditional Assumptions versus Your Legitimate Rights.

   • You may choose to lecture on this topic (see pages 200 to 201). (30 minutes)

   • You may give this as a homework assignment and then divide the class into groups of four to talk about the beliefs people held as children versus as adults. To focus discussion, ask people to comment only on those Legitimate Rights they have difficulty accepting as adults. (15 minutes)

   • You can ask a class member to take a Traditional Assumption position and defend it for a minute. Then ask another student to take the position of the juxtaposed Legitimate Right and defend it for a minute. You can demonstrate how to do this, using the first Traditional Assumption and Legitimate Right in the list. Explain that this may take some play acting for people who are defending positions that they themselves do not hold. As soon as the first Traditional Assumption and Legitimate Right have been presented, move right on to the next. Take questions and comments at the end. If you have ample time, discuss each item as you go. (45 minutes)

4. Describe the Three Basic Interpersonal Styles on page 202 of the workbook.

   • Test your students' ability to distinguish these three styles by asking them to label the six scenes presented on pages 202 to 204. See instruction 3 in the Mini Assertiveness Course of this *Leader's Guide* for suggestions regarding structuring this exercise.

   • Have your students go over their answers to the questions on pages 197 and 199 of the workbook. Follow the instructions in the preceding Mini Assertiveness Course.

5. Tell your students to fill out the Assertiveness Questionnaire on pages 205 to 207 of the workbook. This can be done as homework or classwork. (10 minutes)

6. Explain and demonstrate how to do a problem scene. Have your students write out a description of two to four of their problem scenes, using the instructions on pages 207 to 208 of the workbook. (30 minutes)

   • This can be done as homework or class work.

   • Have students break into groups of two to four in which each person presents one example of a problem scene and the others give constructive feedback. You may want to have people underscore the criteria for a good problem scene on the bottom of page 207, or write these criteria on a blackboard for the small groups to refer to. Have one person report back comments and unanswered questions when the large group reconvenes.

7. "Your Script for Change" (90 minutes)

   - Instructions: See pages 208 to 213 in the workbook.

   - Go over the six steps in the "LADDER."

   - Explain the difference between a poor and good LADDER by using examples.

   - Have individuals write an example of a LADDER based on one of their problem scenes.

   - Break the large group into groups of two or three, and have each individual present his LADDER and get constructive feedback from the listener(s).

   - Have a spokesperson from each of the small groups bring comments and questions back to the large group. This is an important opportunity for you to correct any major misconceptions.

   - Demonstrate how to use the LADDER in a role play between yourself and a class volunteer, or set up a role play between two students, using one of their LADDER scripts.

   - Mention and demonstrate the five basic rules for assertive body language (see page 215 of the workbook).

   - Have each individual in the same small groups role-play their LADDER with one other person, while the other member observes and then gives feedback. The other person in the role play can give valuable information about what it was like to be on the receiving end of the LADDER.

   - Have a spokesperson from each of the small groups bring questions and comments back to the large group.

   - Mention to the group that the LADDER is a valuable tool to use when a person is faced with a major problem scene that she can anticipate, such as asking her boss for a raise or setting limits with a friend. It is also good to use in problem scenes where the individual has a long established pattern of responding nonassertively. In such cases, she can anticipate the problem coming up again, and can think through and rehearse her new assertive response.

   - Have your students practice this technique as homework at least twice and report back. Further role-playing and feedback may be necessary to address problems that have come up.

8. Short Form Assertive Technique (30 to 40 minutes)

   - This technique is particularly useful when you don't have time to prepare your response. It is easy enough to remember to use in almost any situation.

   - Instructions: See pages 214 and 215.

- Point out to your students that the Short Form Assertive Technique is identical to three of the elements in "Your Script for Change":

  "Define the problem" is the same as "I think."

  "Describe your feelings" is the same as "I feel."

  "Express your request" is the same as "I want."

- Demonstrate this technique to the class in a role play, then have your students practice in groups of three or four, and then report back to the large group.

- Have your students practice this technique as homework.

9. Learning How to Listen (30 to 40 minutes)

    - Instructions: See workbook pages 215 to 217.

    - Explain assertive listening.

    - Demonstrate assertive listening in a role play.

    - Have students break into groups of four to role-play assertive listening. The person who is listening should request the speaker to play the role of someone in a situation that the listener would have difficulty listening to in real life.

    - Have the spokesperson from each small group report back to the large group comments and questions.

    - Have your students practice this technique as homework.

10. Arriving at a Workable Compromise (30 to 40 minutes)

    - Instructions: See pages 217 to 218 in the workbook.

    - Explain Workable Compromise.

    - Demonstrate Workable Compromise.

    - Have your students go back to their problem scenes of their LADDER and think about the best way for them to arrive at a Workable Compromise for each one of these scenes.

    - Have your students in groups of four role-play Workable Compromise with one other person, with two people observing and coaching.

    - Have your students practice this technique as homework.

11. Avoiding Manipulation (30 to 90 minutes)

    - Instructions: See pages 218 to 219 in the workbook.

    - Explain each of the seven techniques for dealing with manipulation, giving a brief demonstration of each as you go.

- Mention that two of the dangers in using Content-to-Process Shift are inaccurately reading the other person's mind and appearing condescending.

- Point out that Defusing and Assertive Delay are basically other ways of saying "time out" when you realize the conversation is going nowhere.

- Go over the typical blocking gambits that are used to block assertive requests. Give examples of each and of how to deal assertively with each.

- Note that Assertive Agreement, Clouding, and Assertive Inquiry are three ways of dealing with critics.

- These are fun techniques to practice, using role play.

- The Broken Record and the techniques for dealing with criticism are particularly useful.

Special Note

Whenever you break the larger groups into small groups to work on a specific exercise, you need to circulate around to all of the small groups to be sure that they are focused on the exercise and are doing it correctly. This is also an opportunity to answer questions and hear comments from people too shy to speak up in the large group. When appropriate, encourage these people to bring up their questions and comments in the larger group so that they can practice being assertive.

When you have four to five hours, you can teach everything in the Assertiveness Training chapter in the workbook. Ideally, you should have at least twice that much time, spread out over four to eight weeks. Assertive behavior change involves interacting with significant people in an individual's life. It is helpful when the student can practice an assertive technique during role play in class, and follow this up with an "in vivo" homework assignment. They then can return to the next class session to report on and fine-tune their newly acquired assertive skill. It is also useful when the individuals can read and reflect on the Mistaken Traditional Assumptions versus Your Legitimate Rights so that they are more conscious of what they believe, why they believe as they do, and how this affects their behavior. Finally, it saves class time when students can fill out some of the questionnaires as homework, to be discussed in a later class.

18

Job Stress Management

Introduction

Purpose: Even if most of the people in your class are homemakers or full-time students, they may be suffering from the burnout that comes from chronically not feeling in control of their lives. They would benefit, therefore, from tools designed to empower them. This is the central theme of Job Stress Management.

Time: 5 minutes

Instructions: See pages 221 and 222 of the workbook to introduce this topic.

Ten Steps Toward Managing Your Job Stress

Step 1. Identify Your Symptoms of Job Stress

Time: 8 minutes

Materials: If this is done as class work, you may choose to make copies of the inventory for people to fill out, read the questions, and have them write their answers on a blank piece of paper, or have them fill out the questions in the book.

Instructions: See pages 222 and 223 in the workbook.

Step 2: Identify the Sources of Your Job Stress

Time: 10 minutes

Materials: Either have your students use their own workbook or give them copies of this inventory to fill out.

Instructions: See pages 223 to 226 of the workbook.

Step 3: Identify How You Respond to Your Specific Job Stressors

Time: 40 minutes

Materials: paper and pen

Instructions: See pages 226 to 229 of the workbook.

Note:

- This is a good homework assignment. Students may want to take notes during their workday or at the end of the day.

- Have students discuss their response to stressors in groups of two to four and then report back to the large group.

Step 4: Set Goals to Respond More Effectively to Your Job Stressors

Time: 30 minutes

Materials: piece of paper and pen

Instructions:

1. See pages 229 and 230 in the workbook.

2. Give your students 15 minutes to write a contract.

3 Have students review their contracts in groups of two to four for 10 minutes.

4. Address questions and comments when the large group reconvenes.

Step 5: Motivate Yourself

Time: 5 minutes

Materials: paper and pen

Instructions:

1. See pages 230 and 231 of the workbook.

2. Have your students write several ways that they can reward themselves for working on and achieving their goals.

3. Tell your students to write a more preferred activity that they can use to motivate themselves to do a less preferred activity.

Step 6: Change Your Thinking

Time: 1 hour

Materials: paper and pen

Instructions:

1. See pages 231 to 234 in the workbook.

2. After you have explained the three generic thoughts about work that trigger painful emotions, have your students write examples of each from their own lives on a piece of paper.

3. After you have explained how to cope with the three stressful generic thoughts, have your students write coping statements for each of their stressful thoughts that fall in this category. Then answer any questions.

4. After you have explained how to change or adapt to work stressors, have your students write how they will do this for each of the statements they wrote under this category. Then answer any questions.

5. After you have suggested that class members consider their options and the risk of pursuing these options, have them write options and risks involved for each thought they listed under the third category. Then answer any questions.

6. Have your students meet in groups of two to four and share one generic thought and its coping statement from each of the three categories. Address comments and questions when the large group reconvenes.

Step 7: When in Conflict, Negotiate

Time: 45 to 60 minutes

Materials: paper and pen

Instructions:

1. See page 234 in the workbook.

2. Explain and demonstrate, using role playing, the four steps of negotiation.

3. Have your students write a script to negotiate an office conflict, using this four-part model.

4. Divide your class into groups of four. Let each person take a turn at role playing their script with one other person in the small group. The two observers can act as coaches.

At the end of the role play, have the small group discuss what was good about it, as well as what could be improved.

5. Have the small group reporter share comments and questions when the large group reconvenes.

Step 8. Pace and Balance Yourself

Time: 15 minutes

Materials: paper and pen

Instructions:

1. See pages 235 and 236 in the workbook.

Additional points

2. Have your students read this section, and then write specifically how they could apply each of the eight suggestions to their lives. If an item does not apply, have them write N/A. This can be done as a homework assignment.

3. Have them share their answers in groups of four.

4. Suggest that they apply these ideas to their daily schedule.

19

Nutrition

Introduction

Purpose: To give students the opportunity to compare their usual eating patterns with 10 basic rules for positive eating so that they will be motivated to make improvements in the way that they eat.

Time: 3 minutes

Instructions: Describe the value of healthy eating (see pages 237 to 238 in the workbook).

Self-Assessment

Time: no time to three days of homework; 0 to 25 minutes of class time

Materials: for each student (if they do not have the workbook), a blank copy of the Daily Food Diary (from which they can make at least two additional copies), a copy of Sharon's Food Diary, a copy of Sharon's Food Diary Summary, and a blank copy of the Food Diary Summary

Instructions:

1. See pages 248 to 253 in the workbook.

2. Ideally, you can have your students keep a Daily Food Diary for three days as homework prior to a discussion of the principles of healthy eating. Explain that the purpose of keeping this record is to get an exact account of what they are actually consuming, which they can later compare with what nutrition experts consider a balanced diet.

3. Use Sharon's Food Diary on page 250 of the workbook as an example of how to fill out one day of the Daily Food Diary. The first three columns are self-explanatory, but you still need to remind people to list precisely what they are eating, especially if it contains fat, sugar, or caffeine. The Food Guide Points column is a rough estimate of how to count servings. Go over the bulleted guidelines on page 249 and then use Sharon's Food Diary as an example of how to fill this out. Have your students write down in the Setting column the circumstances in which they were eating and their feelings while they were eating in the Feelings column. The environment in which a person eats and how he feels when eating often influences what he eats. External and internal cues other than hunger often trigger eating. Explain to your students that becoming aware of what they eat as well as what is going on when they eat is the first step toward establishing a healthy diet.

4. At the completion of three days, have your students fill out the blank Food Diary Summary. For each of the three days they kept a food diary, have them add up all the servings in each respective food group. To calculate the *Daily Average* for a food group, add up the servings in days one, two, and three for that food group and then divide by three. They can better compare their Daily Average Servings with the Ideal Servings after they have learned about the Ten Steps to Positive Eating.

5. *Optional:* If you find it necessary to have your students fill out the Daily Food Diary after you have discussed the Ten Steps to Positive Eating, caution your students not to change their eating habits until after they have completed their Daily Food Diary.

6. *Optional:* If it is not possible for your students to keep their Daily Food Diary for three days, have them fill out a blank Daily Food Diary form, describing a "typical day" for themselves. This should take about 10 minutes. Then you can give a lecture on the Ten Steps to Positive Eating. Based on their typical day and the Ten Steps to Positive Eating, they can then fill out their blank Your Personal Positive Eating Goals form on page 255 in the workbook.

7. *Optional:* Your students can skip the self-assessment process and simply listen to your lecture on the Ten Steps to Positive Eating. Based on their memories of their usual eating patterns and the Ten Steps to Positive Eating, they can then fill out their blank Your Personal Positive Eating Goals form.

Ten Steps to Positive Eating

Time: 10 to 45 minutes

Materials: for students without a workbook, a copy of the Recommended Pyramid, the Common Pyramid, and Your Fat Scorecard

Instructions:

1. Give a lecture that is geared to your audience that covers the material on pages 238 to 248 in the workbook. You may prefer to give a formal lecture with questions at the

end. But particularly if you are working with a small group, it can be more interesting to the audience if you invite questions and comments as you go along.

2. Illustrate your points with pictures such as the Recommended Food Pyramid and the Common Food Pyramid.

3. Involve your audience by having them fill out Your Fat Scorecard. You may want to create Your Sugar Scorecard and Your Salt Scorecard, using the tips to limit these items on pages 240 and 241.

4. Be sure to make the connection between exercise and nutrition as the best way to achieve and maintain ideal weight.

Taking Charge of Your Nutritional Well-Being

Time: 15 minutes (using Options 5 or 6 under Self-Assessment) to 1 hour and 30 minutes

Materials: for each student, a completed Food Diary Summary; for students without the workbook, a blank Personal Positive Eating Goals form, Sharon's Food Diary, Sharon's Food Diary Summary, and Sharon's Goal-Setting Chart

Instructions:

1. See pages 249 to 256.

2. Have your students review Sharon's Food Diary Summary and compare her average servings for each food group against the ideal servings. What are her major problem areas? What might she do to solve each of these problems?

3. Have your students review Sharon's Goal-Setting Chart to see what Sharon identified as her major problems and how she decided to solve these problems.

4. Have your students review their own Food Diary Summary and compare their average servings per food group against the ideal servings.

5. Have your students write down on their blank Your Personal Positive Eating Goals form any food group in which their average servings differ from the ideal servings, the specific problem, and a solution that they would be willing to try.

6. Have your students review the "Setting" column on their own Daily Food Diaries. Ask what about the setting in which they ate may have contributed to unhealthy eating. If they have a problem situation that they want to change, instruct them to write it in the "Problem" column of their Your Personal Positive Eating Goals form. How might they realistically improve the circumstances in which they eat? Have them write down their answers in the "solution" column of their Your Personal Positive Eating Goals form.

7. Have your students review the Feeling column on their own Daily Food Diaries. Do their feelings when they eat contribute to unhealthy eating? If they want to work on

this, have them write down their answers in the Problem column of their Your Personal Positive Eating Goals form. How might they realistically improve their feelings when they eat? Have them write down their answers in the Solution column of their Your Personal Positive Eating Goals form.

Final Thoughts

1. Remind your students to make only a few changes in their eating habits at a time, and to give their new habits at least a month to become established before they add any more. Making too many changes at once can be stressful!

2. Suggest that they remind themselves about good nutrition by posting the Recommended Food Pyramid and Your Personal Positive Eating Goals on their refrigerator.

3. Point out the resources on nutrition on pages 257 to 258 in the workbook as well as in their local community.

20

Exercise

Purpose: To provide basic information about how to start and stick with a balanced exercise program to help counter the stress response.

Types of Exercise

Time: 5 to 10 minutes

Instructions:

1. See pages 259 to 260 in the workbook.

2. Give a brief introductory lecture on the three basic categories of exercise: aerobic, stretching, and toning.

3. Describe the general benefits of exercise, emphasizing that these benefits occur only with a commitment to regular practice.

4. Ask for a show of hands from people who are already engaged in some form of regular exercise. Ask these people with their hands up to leave them up if this includes at least 20 minutes of aerobic exercise at the minimum of three times a week. Ask the people with their hands still up to leave them up if they also stretch and warm up before starting and stretch and cool down afterwards. Explain the importance of warming up and cooling down. If you have time, ask these people what their exercise program is.

5. See pages 279 and 280 in the workbook.

Developing Your Own Exercise Program

Sample Exercise Program

Time: about 1 hour

Materials: comfortable clothes and a watch with which to count seconds

Instructions:

1. See pages 276 through 279.

2. Take your students through this sample exercise program.

   A. Modify the length of each part to meet the time restrictions of your class.

   B. Demonstrate as well as describe the proper way to do each stretching and toning exercise before you have your students do it.

   C. Explain target heart rate and how to calculate it. Demonstrate how to take your pulse, using the carotid artery and wrist. Have your students count their resting pulse as you keep time for 10 seconds and then have them multiply this number by 6.

   D. Assume that your class is out of shape and take them through the three-part progressive aerobic section on pages 278 and 279 in the workbook. Have your students continue checking their pulse.

3. *Optional:* Save time by integrating the introduction with this sample exercise program.

Daily Diary of Oppurtunities to Exercise

Time: 30 to 40 minutes

Material: one piece of paper and a pen for each student

Instructions:

1. See pages 267 to 272 in the workbook.

2. Give a few examples of typical barriers to exercise, and then invite your students to share why they can't exercise.

3. For homework, have your students keep a Daily Exercise Diary to uncover all the opportunities they have to exercise during the course of their day, along with their reasons for and against exercising. Use Angela's Diary of Opportunities to Exercise on page 268 in the workbook as an example. This exercise can also be done from memory, but accuracy will be reduced.

4. Confront your students' reasons for not exercising, referring to page 270 in the workbook. Have them turn their "I can't" statements into "I choose not to" statements. Get

them to begin to examine and refute beliefs and fears that keep them from exercising. This can be done in the large group, using examples from the workbook and the class.

5. Explain to your group how to respond to their reasons for not exercising. Use the example on page 271 in the workbook: Angela's Responses to Reasons for Not Exercising. If you have a small group, ask each student to share a couple of her reasons for not exercising and her responses in turn. Give corrective feedback. Instruct your group to complete the blank form Your Responses to Reasons for Not Exercising on page 272. This may be given as homework. If you have a large group, have your students give each other feedback about each others' completed forms in groups of two or three, and then report back to the large group with unanswered questions and with comments.

Choosing the Best Type of Exercise for You (Optional)

Time: 10 minutes

Materials: If your students do not have their own workbook, give them copies of page 273 in the workbook.

Instructions:

1. Have students who want to consider new options for exercises fill in the blanks on page 273 in the workbook.

2. Have your students read about the pros and cons of different types of aerobic exercise on pages 275 and 276 in the workbook.

Establishing Goals

Time: 15 to 30 minutes

Materials: For students who do not have a workbook, a copy of the Sample Contract Form on page 186 and a copy of the Exercise Diary on page 281 in the workbook.

Instructions:

1. See pages 274 to 281 in the workbook.

2. Give a brief lecture describing the basic ingredients of exercise goals. You may want to include some of the ideas from Goal Setting and Time Management, in chapter 16 in the workbook. There is an example of Angela developing an action plan to accomplish a goal involving exercise beginning in the middle of page 183 in the workbook.

3. Have your students fill out a self-contract describing their exercise goals.

4. Suggest that they keep an Exercise Diary.

Special Considerations

Time: 5 to 10 minutes

Instructions:

1. See pages 279 to 280 in the workbook.

2. Give a brief lecture on Avoiding Injury. Invite questions and comments. This is a summary of important precautions that can be skipped if you have already covered them.

3. Most people have difficulty sticking with an exercise program. Keeping at It on page 280 is a summary of suggestions for your students on how to make their exercise program a permanent part of their lives. Skip it if you have already covered these points.

21

When It Doesn't Come
Easy–Getting Unstuck

Introduction

Purpose: To explore why some people are not doing the homework, not applying stress management and relaxation techniques to their daily lives, or not experiencing symptomatic relief.

Instructions:

1. See pages 283 to 286 in the workbook.

2. This topic is optional.

3. Briefly present, in lecture form, the major points in this chapter. You may choose to have your students read the workbook chapter as homework before your lecture.

4. Have your students discuss, in small groups of four, how some of the ideas presented in this chapter might apply to their situation and what they might do to change.

5. Take questions and comments when the large group reconvenes.

Special Notes

The danger of this chapter is that it places the responsibility for change and symptomatic relief on the individual. This can motivate the individual to initiate change from within, rather than wait for a miracle from without. Or it can make a person feel guilty or resigned if he is still unable to relieve his symptoms after significant effort.

It is important for the individual to be patient and to practice these techniques before deciding whether they are beneficial. If symptoms persist after a sincere effort, the individual should seek professional one-on-one help.

22

Homework

Objective

Homework is an essential part of a stress management class or workshop. It is important because:

1. It allows the student to integrate intellectual concepts and techniques into her experience.

2. Only then can the student decide which concepts and techniques are useful to her, and which are not.

3. Through repetition, a new behavior that was at first awkward will begin to feel natural.

4. If the student repeatedly experiences positive feedback in practicing a new behavior, she is likely to continue doing it long after the stress class is over.

Motivation

A major task of the stress management and relaxation instructor is to motivate students to do their homework. In a sense, class time can be looked upon as the time when students come in to get their new homework assignment and report the results of their efforts on the previous assignment. The instructor can enhance homework compliance by:

- explaining the purpose of an assignment;
- describing the homework in simple step-by-step instruction orally and in writing;
- demonstrating the homework using examples;
- giving the students an opportunity to practice any new technique in class and to ask questions before practicing it at home;

- suggesting a minimum expectation for performance, with the understanding that the students can exceed this;

- having students keep a written record of their homework progress, along with any comments and questions; and

- providing time at the beginning of the next session to discuss the homework experience and to ask questions.

Reviewing Assignments

Discussion of the previous week's homework assignment shouldn't take more than 20 minutes. In a relatively small group of eight or less students, the instructor may choose to go around and briefly check with each student on his homework experience. Or the instructor may prefer to save time and encourage group interaction by using the small group format to discuss the homework. Certainly in larger groups, small group feedback is the most efficient way to discuss homework as well as class assignments. An added bonus of using small groups is that everyone will get an opportunity to speak, including those who are shy. If you opt for small groups, circulate around the room to each small group to be sure everyone is on track and to answer questions.

When you opt for the small discussion groups, you need to provide a clear outline of questions to keep the conversation on track. You may also want to give your students these questions in writing. This is particularly useful for people who arrive late. Typical questions include:

1. Did you meet the minimum expectations of the assignment? Did you exceed the minimum expectations?

2. Do you have any questions about the instructions or your experience?

For those who did the assignment:

3. What did you learn from doing this assignment?

4. What did you like and dislike about the assignment?

5. Do you think that you would benefit from continued practice of the ideas and/or techniques you learned in this assignment? Will you continue to practice them?

For those who did not do the assignment:

6. Briefly, why did you not do the assignment? If something else took priority over your homework, what does that mean to you? Is that something that you want to change? If "yes," how can you make the change?

7. Recall why you are here. Do you think that the homework assignment might help you achieve your purpose for being here?

8. Do you want to do this homework assignment this week? If so, what would you decide to do differently this week?

"No" to Homework

It is important for a person to understand why he does not do his homework assignment, since the reasons he gives will tend to reflect how he maintains his stress patterns.

1. If he rarely says "no" to others, he is devoting most of his energy to others and has little time for himself and this stress management homework assignments. He would benefit from the workbook chapters on Assertiveness Training and on Goal Setting and Time Management.

2. If he is a perfectionist, he is likely to set high standards for himself, which he cannot possibly achieve. He may respond to his high standards by not trying, criticizing himself, procrastinating until the last minute, or doing the assignment but not feeling satisfied with his results and not feeling motivated to continue doing the technique beyond the homework assignment. He needs encouragement to set reasonable goals and permission to make mistakes. He would benefit from the workbook chapters on Refuting Irrational Ideas and on Goal Setting and Time Management.

3. If he is an enthusiastic idealist who jumps into the assignment with both feet, he is likely to soon discover that doing the assignment does not net him the instant rewards he hoped for. In fact, by practicing a new behavior excessively, he may create new stress in his life. Disillusioned, he loses interest, and stops. Such is the case with people who go on rigid diets or exercise programs. He needs to be reminded that to keep balance in his life, he must do all things in moderation and be patient. Progress can be slow. While he needs to work steadily, the rewards will not always materialize as quickly as he would like. He would benefit from the Refuting Irrational Ideas and the Goal Setting and Time Management chapters in the workbook.

4. If he is afraid of new experiences, he will tend to interpret any minor problem as a major obstacle that he cannot overcome. Therefore, he is likely to abandon the exercise. If he becomes anxious or has a stressful thought in the middle of a relaxation exercise, he may assume that it is the fault of the exercise. He needs reassurance from the group leader that he is doing the exercises correctly and that the experiences he is having are normal. He also needs permission to be creative in solving little problems that come up in doing the homework. He would benefit from the Refuting Irrational Ideas and Coping Skills chapters in the workbook.

5. If he believes that self-improvement should not involve effort and inconvenience, he is likely to do the class assignments—but not the homework. He needs to be reminded that his old habits took a long time to form, and it stands to reason that he will have to practice a new behavior for a long time before it becomes habitual and natural. In the meantime, new behavior is going to feel awkward, if not downright uncomfortable. Just because a person knows that exercise is good for him does not mean that he will enjoy exercising at first. Only after he has established an exercise pattern in which he can experience its benefits (e.g., improved mood, concentration, physical fitness, and energy) will he be motivated to continue exercising on his own.

6. If he resents being told to do something by anyone, he is likely to resist doing homework assignments. This is a pattern that was probably established early in life, and is unlikely to change in a stress class. As a group leader, take the position that you are responsible for presenting the material, and he can do whatever he likes with it. He is responsible for his own decisions about how he uses his time. If you have good rapport with someone who is oppositional, it is sometimes fun to predict that he won't do the assignment and then be amazed when he does it to spite you. Suggest to people who do not do their assignments and appear not to be improving that one of their options is individual psychotherapy to explore their motivation. Another option is to remind them of their right to stay the same.

7. If he does the homework assignment in a manner that varies significantly from the original instructions, first determine whether the general goal of the assignment was accomplished. If so, compliment him on his creativity and ability to shape the assignment to his own needs. If the general goal of the homework was not reached, point this out and ask him if he is interested in achieving this goal or satisfied with his outcome. If he wants to achieve this goal, have him meet with you or one of the students who was successful with the assignment during the break to go over the instructions and correct his misconceptions.

Here are some additional suggestions for reviewing homework assignments:

- Do not chastise people for not doing their homework. Everybody learns in different ways. Keep in mind that some people will go through the entire class without doing homework and yet appear to benefit from the class. They seem to pick up what they need by attending the class and reading the workbook.

- When someone is conscientiously doing the assignments and yet continues to have significant symptoms of stress, he should be referred for medical and/or psychiatric evaluation.

- In further structuring the small groups, suggest that the people who did not do the assignment report after the people who did do the assignment. This ensures that those who put out the effort to do homework get corrective feedback.

- While it is useful for the individual to understand why he did not do his homework, this should not become the major focus of small group discussion. A person can simply acknowledge to the group that it was his decision not to do the assignment, why he gave priority to something else, and whether this is indicative of a pattern in his life that he could change if he wanted to. Remind people to change "I couldn't . . . " to "I chose not to . . . ." Then he can decide if he wants to do the assignment during the next week, given his personal needs and priorities.

- Ask one person to volunteer to act as a spokesperson for the small group when the large group reconvenes. This person can share with the large group any interesting comments or unanswered questions that came up in the small group.

- Model clearly defined boundaries. Tell your students that you are their stress management and relaxation consultant who will share the most current concepts and techniques available to help them with their stress management problems. Remind students that they are ultimately responsible for their own well-being. You respect their right to do as they choose with their lives, including the decision to remain the same by not doing anything differently. Part of your own personal stress management is not to take responsibility for decisions that are the responsibility of others.

23

Class Formats of Varying Lengths

Three-Hour Presentation

I. *Introduction* (20 minutes)

    A See chapter 1 of workbook: How You React to Stress

    B. What is Stress?

    C. Four Major Sources of Stress

    D. The Fight or Flight Response

    E. Chronic Stress and Disease

    F. Typical symptoms of stress in everyday life

    G. The remainder of this presentation will focus on ways that the average person can gain greater control over the stress in her life.

II. *Take care of your playing piece in the game of life* (1 hour)

    A. Why is it important to take care of your body?

    It is true that your susceptibility to life-threatening illness is largely determined by your ancestry. But while you had no control over who your parents were, you do have some choice about what to do with the body you inherited. Most people who take good care of their bodies say they do so because it makes them feel good and enhances their quality of life. It also makes it easier for them to cope with the daily onslaught of stresses that can slowly wear down a body that is not kept in good condition.

    B. Exercise (10 minutes)

      1. See chapter 20 in the workbook.

2. Briefly describe the basic three types of exercise, their purpose, how frequently they should be practiced, and for what duration.

3. Encourage your group to start and stick with a moderate and safe exercise program.

4. Encourage taking advantage of the many opportunities for exercise they have throughout their day. Give a few examples.

5. Point out some of the typical reasons people give for not exercising (or elicit them from the audience) and then counter these arguments or point out possible solutions for each one of their excuses. Give a few examples and/or elicit them from the audience.

C. Nutrition (10 minutes)

1. See chapter 19 in the workbook.

2. Provide your audience with the Food Diary Summary, which gives their ideal number of daily servings and serving size (see page 253 in the workbook).

3. Briefly go over the Ten Steps to Positive Eating, referring to the Food Diary Summary as appropriate.

4. Encourage your audience to keep track of their food intake for the next three days and then compare their daily average servings with the ideal servings column on the far right of the Food Diary Summary. If they discover any major discrepancies, encourage them to begin making a few changes in their diet at a time.

D. Relaxation (35 to 40 minutes)

1. The Relaxation Response versus the Stress Response (see page 2 of the workbook).

2. Teach the Relaxing Sigh (see page 26 of the workbook).

3. Have your participants get into a comfortable position in their chairs. Tell them to take everything off their lap, and then teach Breathing Awareness and Deep Breathing (see pages 23 to 25 of the workbook, and chapter 3 in this guide). Alternatively, teach Progressive Relaxation.

4. While your participants are still in their relaxed position, have them imagine themselves in their special place (see Creating Your Special Place on page 55 of the workbook).

5. At the end of this exercise, suggest that they now return to the room relaxed, alert, and refreshed. Suggest they practice, on a daily basis, the relaxation exercises they just learned, as well as carry out their plans to improve their exercise and nutrition programs.

6. Suggest that people stand up, stretch, walk around, and take a five-minute break.

7. After the break, answer questions. (5 minutes)

III. *Take charge of your thoughts* (40 minutes)

A. Explain how "man is not disturbed by events, but by the view he takes of them." See pages 107 to 109 in the workbook.

B. Go over the Rules to Promote Rational Thinking (see page 119 in the workbook).

C. Use the exercise Rational Emotive Imagery (see pages 124 and 125 in the workbook) to show your audience how to develop their own strategies for changing stressful emotions by altering their stressful thoughts. Rational Emotive Imagery is the briefest cognitive exercise in the workbook and it can provide your audience with a powerful experience of how thoughts influence feelings.

D. *Optional:* Instead of C, teach how to Refute Irrational Ideas (see pages 119 to 123 in the workbook). Provide your audience with a copy of pages 122 and 123 if they do not have their own copy of the workbook.

E. *Optional:* If students need to work on their anxious thoughts, replace the Rational Emotive Imagery exercise with the Risk Assessment exercise in the Worry Control chapter beginning on page 140 in the workbook. If your students need to work on their angry thoughts, replace the Rational Emotive Imagery exercise with the Create Stress-Coping Thoughts for Anger exercise in the Coping Skills chapter starting on page 166 in the workbook.

IV. *Take an active stance in how you use your time* (50 minutes)

A. Introduce this topic by covering the points described under Background on pages 175 and 176 in the workbook. In particular, explain the 80-20 principle.

B. Introduce the concept of setting priorities by going over Organizing Your Day on pages 194 and 195 of the workbook.

C. Go over 10 of the 12 suggestions for Organizing Your Time on pages 193 and 194 in the workbook. Skip items 2 and 3, which relate to goal setting. Tie in the idea of setting priorities when using their organizer (first suggestion). Save item 6 for last, as it leads into D.

D. Three easy steps to setting limits and asking for what you want. Refer to the Short Form Assertiveness Technique on pages 214 and 215 in the workbook.

V. *Summarize your major points and answer questions* (10 minutes)

One-Hour Presentation

The three-hour format can be shortened to a one-hour presentation as follows:

I. *Introduction* remains the same as in the three-hour presentation (15 minutes)

II. *Take care of your playing piece in the game of life* (15 minutes)

A. Summarize your points about exercise and nutrition in five minutes.

B. Do a 10-minute relaxation exercise of your choice.

III. *Take charge of your thoughts and feelings* (15 minutes)

    A. Summarize how "man is not disturbed by events, but by the view he takes of them" in 5 minutes (see pages 107 to 109).

    B. Go over the Rules to Promote Rational Thinking (see page 119 in the workbook).

    C. Give an example of Rational Emotive Imagery to show your audience how to change their stressful emotions by altering their stressful thoughts (see pages 124 to 125 in the workbook).

IV. *Be proactive in organizing your time, setting limits, and asking for what you want.* (15 minutes)

    A. Same as IV A and B in the preceding three-hour presentation

    B. Summarize the 3 easy steps to setting limits and asking for what you want.

V. *Save five minutes at the end to summarize your major points and answer questions.*

Ten-Week Class

You can introduce topics from all of the chapters in the workbook in a ten-week stress management class. Be realistic. Do not try to teach every exercise, as students need time to practice them between sessions to benefit, and you don't want to overload them. When the workbook was first published, the general rule of thumb was to teach one stress management chapter and one relaxation chapter each week. It is clear today that depending on the needs of your group, you may want to spend more time on certain topics and go lightly over or skip others. You can use the Symptom Effectiveness Chart on pages 12 and 13 in the workbook to help you decide which chapters you want to emphasize.

    Some techniques such as Applied Relaxation, Worry Control, and Coping Skills integrate techniques from other chapters and therefore should be taught later in the class schedule. Because these three chapters include multiple techniques that build upon one another and that students need to practice between sessions, they need to be taught over several weeks if they are to be taught in their entirety.

    There are a variety of ways to introduce topics without expending a lot of class time on them. For instance, you can assign chapter 11, Recording Your Own Relaxation Tape, as home reading and then demonstrate its major points in the class session in which you teach the basic procedure of Progressive Relaxation or Hypnosis. You can combine two stress management chapters around a common theme. For instance, it makes sense to teach nutrition and exercise in one session under the title of "taking care of your body." You can teach one of the thought stopping techniques or one of the brief combination relaxation exercises when you discover you have completed your material for a session fifteen minutes early.

    The following is a suggested ten-week Relaxation and Stress Reduction Class format:

Week	Relaxation Exercise	Stress Management Technique
1	Body Awareness	Introduction
2	Breathing	Nutrition and Exercise

3	Visualization	Refuting Irrational Ideas
4	Progressive Relaxation & Recording Your own Relaxation Tape	Thought Stopping
5	Applied Relaxation Training	Goal Setting & Time Management
6	Applied Relaxation Training	Assertiveness Training
7	Autogenics	Worry Control
8	Meditation	Coping Skills
9	Self-Hypnosis	Job Stress Management
10	Brief Combinations	When It Doesn't Come Easy – Getting Unstuck

12-Hour Workshop in Two Days

Day 1

I. *Introduction* (1 hour and fifteen minutes)

A. Have your students purchase the text, *The Relaxation & Stress Reduction Workbook*, as part of the price of your workshop.

B. See chapter 1 of the workbook: How You React to Stress, and chapter 1 of this guide: Introduction to Relaxation and Stress Reduction.

C. Introduce yourself, describing your background, especially as it relates to stress management, and why you are teaching this workshop. Have group members introduce themselves and state why they are there. If the group is large, break into dyads.

D. Hand out an outline of your workshop, listing topics to be covered and when people can expect breaks.

E. Define stress.

F. Describe the four major sources of stress.

G. Explain the Fight or Flight Response and the Relaxation Response.

H. Explain the relationship between chronic stress and disease.

I. Exercise: Schedule of Recent Experience (30 minutes)
See pages 3 to 6 in the workbook and see chapter 1 in this guide.

J. Exercise: Symptoms Checklist
See pages 7 and 8 in the workbook.

K. Exercise: Tactics for Coping with Stress Inventory
See pages 8 to 10 in the workbook.
(15-minute break)

II. *Take care of your playing piece in the game of life* (1 hour and 30 minutes)

   A. Why is it important to take care of your body?

      1. Nature versus nurture issue

      2. Taking control of what you can

      3. Quality of life

      4. Better prepared to cope with adversity as well as normal aging

   B. Exercise (40 minutes)

      1. See chapter 20 in the workbook and chapter 20 in this guide.

      2. Describe the three basic forms of exercise, why they are important, and how frequently and for what duration they need to be done to experience their benefit.

      3. Lead your group through an exercise including the stretching and toning exercises on pages 262 to 265 in the workbook.

      4. Teach about resting heart rate and target heart rate and how to determine it (see pages 277 to 279 in the workbook). After they have taken their resting heart rate, have them walk briskly in place for a minute and then have them take their pulse again.

      5. Briefly explain how they can safely start a regular exercise program that fits who they are and stick with it. Refer to chapter 20 in the workbook. Optional: Have your group break into dyads and discuss their current exercise program or an exercise program that they would like to start. Encourage them to include all three types of exercise in their own program.

      6. Daily Opportunities to Exercise

         a. See pages 267 to 272 in the workbook. Here is a brief way to present this material:

         b. Explain how even short periods of exercise are healthful, and how we all have many chances to exercise throughout our day that we pass up. Give a couple of examples, such as stairs versus elevators, and elicit a few more from your audience.

         c. We pass up these opportunities for reasons that seem reasonable at the time. Give some examples and elicit a few more from your audience.

         d. We know that these reasons are often excuses and that by expending a little energy we could take advantage of many of these opportunities to exercise, if only for a few minutes. But this would mean pushing through our excuses, something we are unwilling to do when we are tired or preoccupied with other things. Give some examples of confronting excuses, and elicit a few more from the audience.

C. Deep Relaxation (20 minutes)

Teach Breathing Awarensess and Deep Breathing (see pages 23 to 25 of the workbook and chapter 3 in this guide).

D. Nutrition (40 minutes)

1. See chapter 19 in the workbook and guide.

2. Exercise: Have your students write from memory what they typically ingest during the course of a day, in the appropriate categories on the Food Diary Summary (see page 253 in the workbook).

3. Summarize the Ten Steps to Positive Eating, referring to the Food Diary Summary as appropiate.

4. Exercise: Have your students write down at least three ways that they would like to improve their diet and suggest that they set these as goals for the next two weeks.

(lunch break)

III. *Take charge of your time* (1 hour)

A. Introduce this topic by covering the points described under Background on pages 175 and 176 in the workbook. In particular, explain the 80-20 principle.

B. Introduce the concept of setting priorities by going over Organizing Your Day on pages 194 and 195 of the workbook.

C. Go over ten of the twelve suggestions for Organizing your Time on pages 193 and 194 in the workbook. Skip or rephrase items two and three, which relate to goal setting. Tie in the idea of setting priorities when using their organizer (first suggestion).

D. Instruct your students to write out how they plan to spend one of their next days off, using some of the suggestions given.

E. Have your group write down a few things they have been putting off doing and then go over the section on Combating Procrastination on pages 191 to 193 in the workbook.

G. Tell the individuals in your group to write down how they could motivate themselves to get done the things they wrote they were putting off doing. Have them discuss their plans in dyads.

IV. *Be assertive* (2 hours)

A. Teach the difference between Aggressive, Passive, and Assertive Communication. Give examples, and demonstrate the body language of each of these three types of communication.

B. Teach three easy steps to setting limits and asking for what you want (see Short Form Assertiveness Technique on pages 214 and 215). Have students role-play for practice.

C. (Optional) Explain and demonstrate assertive listening (see pages 215 and 216 in the workbook). Have students role-play for practice.

D. (Optional) Summarize the concept of workable compromise (see pages 217 and 218 in the workbook) and demonstrate an example, using role play. Point out that for a workable compromise to have a chance of being successful, you need to use both your assertive expressing skills and assertive listening skills. Have students role-play with everyone being assertive for practice.

E. Prepare your students for real life by teaching them how to avoid manipulation (see pages 218 to 219 in the workbook). Have students role-play for practice as time permits.

Day 2

V. *Take charge of your thoughts*

A. Explain how "man is not disturbed by events, but by the view he takes of them." (5 minutes)
(See pages 107 to 109 of the workbook.)

B. Go over at least the first 10 of the 21 Irrational Beliefs. (30 minutes)
(See pages 115 to 119 in the workbook and chapter 14 of this guide.)

C. Go over the Rules to Promote Rational Thinking. (3 to 5 minutes)
(See page 119 in the workbook.)

D. Teach steps A through E for Refuting Irrational Ideas. (30 to 40 minutes)
(See pages 119 to 123 in the workbook and chapter 14 of this guide.)
(15-minute break)

E. Teach Progressive Relaxation. (20 minutes)
(See pages 31 to 33 in the workbook and chapter 4 in this guide.)

F. Teach Rational Emotive Imagery. (30 minutes)
(See pages 124 to 125 in the workbook and chapter 14 of this guide.)
(5-to-10 minute break)

G. Teach one of the Thought Stopping techniques. (20 to 30 minutes)
(See pages 127 to 133 in the workbook and chapter 13 of this guide.)
(1 hour lunch break)

H. Teach Coping Skills for Anxiety or Anger. (1 hour and 15 minutes)
(See pages 151 to 174 in the workbook and chapter 15 of this guide.)
(10-minute break)

VI. *Teach Self-Hypnosis.* (1 hour and 15 minutes)

A. See pages 69 to 82 in the workbook and chapter 8 of this guide.

B. The following is a time-efficient outline:

1. Introduction: In describing the benefits of hypnosis, emphasize deep relaxation and increased openness to positive, healthful suggestions.

2. Demonstrate suggestibility by taking your class through an exercise on postural sway.

3. Teach the elements of good hypnotic suggestions. Give several examples of hypnotic suggestions for relaxation and stress management. Have your students write out three suggestions for themselves to use during the basic self-induction exercise.

4. Describe the basic elements of a hypnotic induction as well as deepening techniques.

5. Take them through the basic self-induction script on pages 73 and 74 in the workbook, which includes the basic elements and deepening techniques that you described.

6. Invite comments and questions on self-hypnosis.

VII. *Summary* (15 minutes)

A. Highlight the important points that you presented in your introduction the first day.

B. Show your students how to use the Symptom Effectiveness Chart on pages 12 and 13 in the workbook.

C. Stress that practice of these techniques on a regular basis for at least a month will help to establish habits of effective stress management and relaxation.

D. Invite questions and comments.